FOR FRANCHISE
LEADERS
EYES ONLY

FOR FRANCHISE
LEADERS
EYES ONLY

Shape Your Network's Future With A Proven Growth Leadership System

STEPHANE BREAULT
FRANCHISE EXPERT & EXECUTIVE COACH

Imagine Franchise

Montréal, Canada

Imagine Franchise Consultant Inc.
200 André Prévost, suite 408
Montreal, Quebec, Canada, H3E 0E5
www.imaginefranchise.com
sbreault@imaginefranchise.com

For Franchise Leaders Eyes Only, Stephane Breault —1st ed.

CERTIFIED

(H)

WRITTEN
BY HUMAN

Testimonials

What Do They Think of the Book?

"Drawing on his depth of experience leading and guiding franchise systems, Stéphane provides practical and actionable guidance. This valuable read is for those looking to achieve excellence in franchising."

Brian Leon
Chief Executive Officer, Choice Hotels Canada

"As the owner of the Local Handyman Group, I've witnessed firsthand the challenges and opportunities inherent in the franchising world. *For Franchise Leaders Eyes Only* by Stéphane Breault arrives as an essential tool for anyone at the helm of a franchise operation. Breault masterfully simplifies complex ideas into actionable insights that resonate deeply with those of us committed to the success of our networks.

The book is exceptionally well-written—clear, concise, and direct, with each chapter providing strategic knowledge that's easy to digest and implement. From unraveling the intricacies of growth leadership to fostering operational excellence, Breault doesn't shy away from the hard truths that many of us face but need to hear. This book stands out because of its practical framework, which feels like navigating a clear path in the often-tumultuous journey of franchise management.

I highly recommend *For Franchise Leaders Eyes Only* to current and aspiring franchise leaders. The lessons here are not just theoretical but grounded in the reality of running a franchise day-to-day. It's a book that promises not just to inform but to transform your approach, ensuring your franchise is not only surviving but thriving in today's competitive market."

Nathan Neels
Owner, The Local Handyman Group

"Stéphane Breault's book is packed with valuable insights into the common pitfalls and challenges new franchisors face as they grow their system. His candid approach to sharing real-world lessons is something I wish I had access to when starting out. It's a must-read for anyone looking to build a successful franchise with eyes wide open to the realities of growth."

John Evans
Founder & Chief Executive Officer,
EverLine Franchising Ltd.

"Stéphane Breault brings simple and enthusiastic clarity to the often-complex world of franchise leadership. His book is a powerful guide for navigating the challenges of aligning brands, operations, and values. With practical advice and real-world insights, this resource empowers leaders to make confident decisions. It's essential reading for anyone serious about growing a successful franchise network."

Pino Di Ioia
CEO, Beaver Tails

"I recently had the pleasure of reviewing *For Franchise Leaders Eyes Only*, by Stéphane Breault. From the very first line in the introduction, 'You are 100% responsible for the results you achieve,' I knew this book was going to resonate with me—and it did not disappoint. What I appreciated most was the direct, no-nonsense approach. The book isn't filled with fluff or theory—it's a roadmap for any leader who is ready to embrace their own power and take control of their results. It challenges the reader to reflect deeply on their mindset and habits while providing the tools to transform both."

Ken LeBlanc
President, Propertyguys.com

"Stéphane Breault's combination of research, understanding, and franchise experience for many years is why *For Franchise Leaders Eyes*

Only is such a strong must-read. As a leader in the Canadian Franchise community as President and CEO of The UPS Store Canada and Past Chair of The Canadian Franchise Association, I can say with certainty that Stéphane has created a must-read for our community. Both in theory and in practice, he has created a leadership must-read."

David Druker
CEO, The UPS Store Canada

"I first met Stéphane Breault more than two decades ago, while serving together on the board of The Canadian Franchise Association. I was impressed by his candor, and his ability to be direct. His inherent ability to see things from the other person's point of view, coupled with an uncommon, unlimited amount of common sense, enables him to be able to relate to franchisors and franchisees alike.

Stéphane possesses a unique combination of interpersonal skills and a well-grounded, fundamental understanding of franchising. I have consulted with Stéphane on several franchising issues, always leaving with a better perspective and more enlightened. I wish him every success with this book, and I'm proud to call him my friend."

Murray Oxford
President and CEO, Janiking Canada

Stéphane Breault's new book is a pragmatic approach to franchising that takes his realistic model and drives home the hard lessons that it takes to be successful in this rewarding but challenging industry. Stéphane is a thought leader in our industry and has worked to help brands achieve tremendous success. I believe his strongest message is, you will get out of this based on what you put into it and those words ring true throughout the industry.

Shawn Saraga
Founder – The Franchise Academy, Broker – Revel Realty
Chief Development Officer – Tahini's Restaurants

GET THE BONUS PACKAGE OF *FOR FRANCHISE LEADERS EYES ONLY*.

SCAN THE QR CODE

OR VISIT

https://imaginefranchise.com/en/get-your-ebook-guide-now/
to get access to the bonus package of *For Franchise Leaders Eyes Only* by Stéphane Breault.

You'll discover practical tools that will change the way you lead your network.

Dedication

I dedicate this book to all my clients, past and present. Their courage, experiences, and open-mindedness have been endless sources of inspiration for me. Thanks to them, I have not only grown but also brought this work, which is so dear to my heart, to life. This book is as much the product of their dreams as it is of my thoughts.

To Steve Gordon and his team, Diane Stehle, Tracey-Lee Batsford, and Jennifer Thiboutot, I want to express my deepest gratitude. Your unwavering support and conviction throughout this journey made it possible. Your commitment and trust have been guiding lights along this creative path.

To my wife, Ambre, I can never thank you enough. Your steadfast love and constant support, even in moments when I doubted myself, have been the foundation I could lean on. You have been my refuge and my light in times of uncertainty. It is because of you that this project, so close to my heart, has come to life.

I would also like to pay tribute to my former employers, who, throughout my executive career, allowed me to be bold and challenge the status quo, even when it seemed impossible. Their faith in my vision has shaped the leader I am today.

I wrote this book with a deep intention: to help all franchise leaders grow so that they and their franchisees can fully realize the economic and human potential of their networks.

Stéphane

CONTENTS

PART 3: PRACTICAL CASE STUDIES – THE BEST AND THE WORST

Introduction

"You are 100% responsible for the results you achieve."

-Stéphane Breault

"What you are today is the result of your past choices. What you will be tomorrow will be the result of choices you make today."

-Unknown

Becoming an outstanding franchise leader is like navigating the high seas. It's not a skill that can be learned from a textbook or perfected overnight. The stakes are high, and in franchising, every misstep can be financially disastrous. Imagine this scenario: you're at the helm of a vast network of 100 franchisees. Every mistake you make has repercussions on each franchisee, increasing the likelihood of financial loss, reputational damage, and so on. Again, the stakes are high.

Consider this alarming fact: according to an in-depth MIT Sloan Management Review study, 75% of new franchisors had disappeared into oblivion just 12 years after starting their businesses.[1] What is the main reason behind these failures?

---

[1] https://sloanreview.mit.edu/article/factors-for-new-franchise-success/

None other than poor franchisee performance. In simpler terms, franchisors' leadership—or lack thereof—paved the way for these unfortunate downfalls.

All too often, franchisors who are just starting out are caught up in the magical thinking of franchising: sell the franchise to whoever wants it and train the franchisee to make the franchise work. Then, the franchisee is more or less on their own. Quite simply, it's a recipe for disaster. All this is because the new franchisor hasn't understood that franchising can't survive improvisation, lack of discipline, and inadequate support.

That's why this book focuses on the importance of growth leadership. This is how you can achieve your goals. And these goals are:

Wealth creation: Most franchisors own networks with less than 100 franchisees. The economics of franchising reveal an irrefutable truth: a franchisor with fewer than 100 franchisees typically has a valuation of just three to four times its EBITDA. Franchisors with over 100 franchisees generate valuations of six to 12 times their EBITDA. The message is crystal clear: growth is critical.

A stronger brand: Imagine a franchisor who nurtures an unwavering culture of excellence and empowers their franchisees to be great leaders. This powerful combination creates a brand that stands out and thrives in a fiercely competitive market. The company shines through and acquires more long-term customers.

Less risk: Costly mistakes, underperforming franchisees, and problems in a franchise's ecosystem can prevent even the most robust company from growing. But effective leadership acts as a stabilizing force, a lighthouse that guides the way through the darkest storms. It's the compass that keeps the franchise network on track and sailing smoothly.

In the world of franchising, your success depends on striking the right balance. While the franchise business model undeniably contributes its share, the other 50% of the equation is rooted in the quality of your leadership. To underestimate this vital factor is to abandon the steering wheel, miss opportunities for growth, give up on building a first-rate team, and resign yourself to enduring a relentless whirlwind of chaos. And, as many of us know, chaos is rarely profitable.

Remember this: As the leader of your network, you are 100% responsible for the results you achieve.

As you prepare to embark on this enlightening journey through the pages of this book, remember this: your evolution as a franchise leader is not just a nice-to-have, it's a must. Your franchise network's fate, financial prosperity, and reputation are at stake. This book will be your guide through the ups and downs of franchising. It will provide you with insights, strategies, and a roadmap to make your journey to success easier and exceptional.

Part 1

Leadership and Growth Go Hand in Hand

Chapter 1

Franchising: A Formidable Strategy for Growth That Too Often Falls Flat

When I visit franchise trade shows or attend events involving franchisors, I often ask the question, "How's the growth going?" I get these types of responses:

- It's not so great. I can't find any good candidates.
- It's up and down; the situation is unstable.
- I only manage to open one or two franchises a year—and that's when things are going well.
- We take two steps forward, one step back, and one step sideways. Not much progress.
- Things are going very well, we're getting dozens of leads a month. I've hired three salespeople to keep up with demand. We're on a roll, so we'll see what happens.
- We're opening franchises wherever we have a candidate with the money. We're running around like crazy.

As you can see, growth is often a real issue—and the consequences can be devastating:

1. Loss of opportunity: you can't generate the profits you hoped for.
2. A lack of mobilization both within your organization and among franchisees; everyone loses focus and energy.
3. Damage to your most valuable asset: a brand that isn't growing isn't healthy. The effects of an aging brand can be slow and steady—or extremely fast.
4. Business risk is rising because stagnation has set in: with no new markets and no growth, you're condemned to activate your survival mode. Profits decline. Your ability to innovate and renew is lackluster, to say the least.

Does this resonate with you?

The truth is that most franchisors don't even have ten franchisees up and running after five years.

Why is the situation so fragile?

I have observed three main reasons:

1. The franchisor's lack of investment in growth.
2. Growth is not a team project.
3. You lack focus.

Reason 1: The Franchisor's Lack of Investment in Growth

Too often, franchisors underestimate the investment needed to generate sustained growth. The initial franchise fee collected is used to maintain cash flow from operations, rather than being fully reinvested to boost growth over the long term. Recruiting, selecting the right franchisee, and getting a new franchisee up and running quickly and profitably is expensive. **Not doing so is even more expensive**, because your new franchisees will provide you with revenue growth (royalties, volume discounts, advertising funds) and if they don't achieve results quickly, they won't be able to afford these costs, destroying your franchise's value-creation potential. I'm not even mentioning the fact that they won't be ambassadors for your brand if they don't quickly reap the benefits of their investment.

The ROI of market development is not measured by the amount of initial franchise fees collected but by the value generated by recurring royalties and other revenues.

Let's take a simple example to illustrate the point.

ABC Franchise:

> Initial fee: $35,000
> Annual sales: $1M
> Royalties: 5%
> Other revenues (volume discounts, etc.): 3%
> Total annual recurring revenues for the franchisor: $80,000

First-year investment for a new franchise

Recruitment advertising: $5,000

Development team (salaries and other direct costs): $15,000

Franchisor's start-up support (local advertising, product freebies, etc.): $20,000

Additional investment to support rapid sales growth (special promotions, local advertising reinvestment, product discounts, additional operational coaching, etc.) - Year 1: $25,000

Annual indirect support (franchise success coach, training, and head office general expenses allocation): $40,000

Clearly, the first year is crucial, and if the start-up is well managed, the cost of maintaining it in subsequent years will be lower. Assuming an annual support cost of 50% of collected royalties, the example below demonstrates the positive cash flow created by a well-launched franchise.

Five-year cash flow analysis*

*Organic growth not taken into account.

	Year 1	Year 2	Year 3	Year 4	Year 5
Revenue	$115,000	$80,000	$80,000	$80,000	$80,000
Expenses	$100,000	$40,000	$40,000	$40,000	$40,000
Cash flow generated	$15,000	$40,000	$40,000	$40,000	$40,000
Total cash flow over 5 years	$175,000				

Consider this: the franchisor doesn't directly invest their own money into the creation of a franchise. Instead, they use the initial entry fee and a portion of the first year's royalties to fuel initial growth. When you factor in that the cost of this support is only equivalent to a maximum of 50% of the royalties and other revenues collected, the return on investment for this franchise skyrockets to an astonishing 175,000% over five years. Clearly, investing in growth isn't just wise—it's incredibly lucrative. I'm sure you'll agree that such an investment strategy pays off handsomely.

Reason 2: Growth is Not a Team Project

The growth of a franchise network depends on several factors: the business model, the quality and reputation of the brand, and finally, the franchisor's investment in growth, systems, and support. But that's not all. Indeed, one of the most important levers for attracting and converting prospects into new franchisees, or enabling an existing franchisee to acquire a new location, is trust in the franchisor.

And this confidence comes from external factors such as those mentioned above, but also from internal factors. It's by focusing on the latter that the franchisor's team can make a major difference.

Success in franchising is the result of everyone's efforts. The same applies to growth. Entrusting recruitment and selection to the development team alone, and not involving the rest of the team, is like trying to win a car race without the engineers, mechanics, and other specialists.

The key: Think in terms of a partnership, not a transaction

One of the dangers I see on a regular basis is that franchise development people become franchise salespeople, not experts who help future business partners and brand ambassadors (franchisees) make the best decisions for themselves and the organization. It's a common mistake to "sell" a franchise like you sell real estate. The franchisee is seen as a captive customer who will receive services from the franchisor. But with this vision, we only consider the transactional part of the business. This is not the kind of relationship that can make a network powerful and create value. **Because it's the commitment of franchisees and the franchisor's team to making the partnership work that will make the difference—not the initial transaction.**

But who should be involved in growth, and what role should everyone play in boosting confidence?

The CEO plays three major roles in a franchise's growth. They must:

1. Be the #1 brand promoter.
    It's the CEO's job to communicate the power of the franchise. For example, some CEOs actively participate in social media, podcasts, brand-building activities, or business awards.

2. Ensure that the acquisition of new talent (franchisees and head office employees) corresponds to:
    a. The brand's DNA
    b. The company's vision and mission
    c. Corporate values

And all this, without any compromises.

I'd like to draw your attention to the importance of this last point. You need to see each new franchisee as a strategic acquisition, to avoid the all-too-familiar setbacks experienced by franchisors who fail to pay attention to these points. In fact, you should regard the acquisition of a new franchisee as an investment in your growth as important as a new building or piece of equipment. Here, it's the long-term vision that prevails.

3. Make the whole team accountable for the results of growth—not just the development team.
   Here's how members of the management team should participate in growth.

   VP of Finance: Helps the qualified franchisee understand the investment, run the business to ensure the right control to achieve profitability, and prepare the business plan for financing.

   VP of Franchising: Provides the prospect with the right information and helps them move forward throughout the process, ensuring that everything is done in the interests of both parties (franchisee/franchisor).

   VP of Real Estate & Construction: Playing a crucial role in the franchise's ROI, they maximize profitability by finding the best location at the best price. They also ensure that the construction project is carried out in line with the business model investment.

VP of Marketing: A strategic position; they are responsible for creating excitement around the opening of the new franchisee and supporting the startup plan by acquiring new customers.

VP of Franchisee Success: They contribute to value creation; their responsibilities go far beyond the numbers and operations. They share know-how not only on technical aspects but also on how to succeed as CEO of a new company. They also ensure that the franchisee fully embraces the franchisor's values and initiatives.

Existing franchisees: They're your ambassadors! Make sure they know they're part of the team to grow the network. Train them to be ambassadors for the franchise, and encourage them to refer prospects to you. They need to be involved in your selection process and may become mentors to new franchisees.

In a nutshell, viewing franchise growth as a simple sales process driven by the development team generates neither synergy nor mutual trust. The optimal (if not the fastest) way to achieve growth is to involve the entire management team in the process of acquiring the best talent (franchisees). This will make it easier to create and maintain sustained growth.

Imagine yourself at the helm of a team actively involved in your company's growth. You'll see that:

1. Prospects' and franchisees' confidence will grow, as they see that success isn't just about one person.

2. Each team member's skills will be further developed, as everyone learns from one another.
3. Growth will be easier and less chaotic because everyone will be mobilized to succeed and happy to work on achieving results.

Reason 3: You Lack Focus

1. **New franchisees anytime, everywhere.**
   Imagine this scene:

   You receive a request for information via your website. The prospect seems interesting and lives more than 300 miles from your nearest franchise. You don't know this market, and until this prospect came along, you had absolutely no interest in it. But because you have a prospect, you think the idea of setting up a franchise there would be a good idea. You contact the person, and off you go!

   Sound familiar? Unfortunately, it's the approach of many franchisors. Improvisation leads to incongruities that get in the way of creating the impact you're looking for.

2. **Launching new innovations and projects without checking the economic payback and implementation challenges.**
   Good intentions. Iffy results. In fact, many projects fail because franchisees don't buy into them. Improvisation creates way too many ups and downs and franchisors lose the respect and trust of franchisees. It also delays or kills value creation.

3. **You underestimate the importance of organic growth.**

   a. **Multi-unit franchising**

   Franchisees' potential to grow their business by developing other franchises should not be underestimated. Unfortunately, all too often, franchisors fail to ensure that existing franchisees develop the knowledge and skills that will enable them to grow their business by acquiring a second or more franchises. All too often, multi-unit franchisees arrive at a network by chance, with no real preparation. They take two business risks:

   1. The risk of starting a new business
   2. The risk of losing control and under-performing in all their units.

   If you've had any experience with franchising, you're probably familiar with this common scenario: the super-successful franchisee with one franchise who totally fails after acquiring a few more—all with the approval of the franchisor (who, let's face it, didn't do their job properly).

   b. **Organic sales growth**

   By failing to plan for organic growth, the franchisor deprives themself of an extremely powerful asset of value creation. Indeed, the effect of "same-store sales growth" is a direct source of profit for both parties.

It's easy to understand: ten franchises growing by 10% a year is like opening a new franchise but without all the associated expenses. Pure profit!

4. **You underestimate the importance of ensuring the success of each new franchisee.**
Taking on new franchisees that are quickly profitable is vital to a network. Everyone agrees on this point. So why so many failures? Why are so many new franchisees marginally profitable and fail to create real value for both parties? Here again, we find ourselves faced with the phenomenon of performance anxiety due to the absence of a solid, disciplined growth system. Because that's the thing: it takes discipline to build a solid plan and execute it.

For example: one of my customers has a valid territory optimization study with a potential of 148 franchisees. The leaders have chosen to develop the network from their base (in a specific region) and not to agree to develop another region until the first is at 80% of its potential. The reason for this strategic choice is simple: to achieve success through impact. It's a safe bet that they'll achieve slightly slower growth, but that it will quickly pay off. By being disciplined, they will create growth both internally and externally.

Here are the main consequences of a lack of focus

1. *Limited wealth creation*
   Whether it's the franchisee or the franchisor, business risks increase because decisions are made without an overall view. They are also too often focused on the short term.

2. *Franchisees resistant to change*
   Surprises are rarely welcome for any entrepreneur. Improvising in the face of change is fundamentally disrespectful to your business partners. Want to minimize resistance to change? Plan ahead!

3. *Getting off to a bad start*
   As an expert, I often see franchise location openings that are completely made up as the business goes along. The results are good one day, bad the next, and well below expectations. And yet, the beginning is critical for the franchisee. This is definitely not the time to improvise.

4. *Repetition of basic errors*
   By failing to plan for growth, franchisors don't learn from their mistakes. As a result, mistakes are often repeated, jeopardizing wealth creation not only for franchisees but also for the franchisor—not to mention the mobilization of network resources.

5. *Damage to the most important asset: The brand*
   Over time, improvisation erodes the clear advantages and integrity of the brand. The result: consumers are confused.

In franchising, a strong brand requires discipline and planning, not improvisation and carelessness.

In fact, improvisation due to a lack of focus leads to failure... period.

The leadership team is then unable to plan and execute its decisions properly.

That's my observation, without wanting to judge anyone. Most franchisors don't have an organized growth plan because they don't have an organized growth leadership system. They misunderstand the benefits of planning their growth.

Think planning your growth isn't important? What do you want to experience?

1. *Lots of action, little results:* everyone's working hard, but the profits just aren't there. What do you think your franchisees or team members are going to do? How will you continue?

2. *Too many mistakes kill confidence:* what's your failure rate? Yes, let's talk about it. Too often, it's improvisation that causes a franchisee to fail. Whose fault is that?

3. *The potential of "good" franchisees is restrained, to say the least:* your "good" franchisees aren't fooled; they suffer from your lack of planning. This doesn't help them grow successfully. This quickly discourages them. They'll sell out, and you'll lose out on partners crucial to your success.

The choice is yours.

In Chapters 4 to 10, I'll introduce you to the Imagine Franchise growth leadership system, which I use in a highly personalized way with my clients. It was developed from my experience of over 25 years as a franchise leader and 15 years as an executive coach with franchisors.

One of the aims of this book is to inspire you to change your approach. I recommend that you have a pen and paper handy to take notes or answer the questions I ask. The Coach's Thoughts serve to make the shared material concrete.

Important! By writing on paper, you can be more creative. Make the most of it! It's all about you and your business.

Coach's Thoughts

This is all theory, you may say. Yes, you're right. If you don't do anything about it, nothing will change. So take a few minutes to answer the following questions. Then, you can start to change your strategy for achieving growth.

Q1: How do you feel about your growth? What feelings come to mind when you consider your growth strategy?

Q2: Why do you want to grow your network?

Q3: Define your plan for achieving growth within the next 10 years.

- Which markets do you target?
- How many franchise locations do you intend to have?
- How do you see the head office team evolving?
- What changes will take place within the franchise team?
- What income do you expect?
- How much do you estimate the franchisor's profit to be?
- What is the median EBITDA of your franchise network?
- What is the median ROI of your franchisees?

(**Note:** The median represents the midpoint of a data set, where 50% of units have values less than or equal to the median, and 50% have values greater than or equal to it. The average is the arithmetic average of a series of numbers).

Q4: What will be the consequences if you don't grow (on you, on your team, on your company, and on your franchisees)? Put a price tag on it.

Q5: What benefits will you derive from your growth (be specific, name several benefits that seem important to you)?

Q6: What are the three **MAJOR** decisions you need to make **NOW** to achieve the growth you want?

Chapter 2

Stuck in Neutral: When Franchisors and Franchisees Do Not Work as a TEAM

Being the leader of a franchise network is a major challenge that can't be overcome alone. Success in franchising depends on the team you build. Sounds obvious, right? Yet there are so many challenges to engaging franchisees with the brand. Why is it so hard to find people (your team) who are as committed to the network's success as you are? Why are you unable to reach your growth targets?

In fact, the challenge of creating a committed and dedicated team lies in three factors which, when they work together, act like a turbo effect to promote growth.

1. Creating a franchisor-franchisee team with a common DNA
2. Demonstrating character
3. Master assertive communication to transform your results and boost growth

You have to open your eyes.

Failing to create a high-performance franchisee-franchisor team has many consequences:

1. No local commitment from franchisees: Franchisees are not very involved in their franchise businesses, and under-optimize the potential of their primary markets.
2. Substantial direct costs: The franchisor must build an organization to support and closely monitor franchisees. This means a large team is focused on controlling, not growth.
3. No operational excellence: The result is a loss of quality and a ho-hum customer experience, which doesn't foster customer loyalty and slows growth.

Creating a Franchisor-Franchisee Team With a Common DNA

Team DNA goes far beyond mere marketing slogans. In a franchise network, defining the team's DNA is not as simple as it sounds. There's a fundamental concept to respect: defining a clear alignment. Once properly communicated within the network, this lays the foundations for the brand's DNA.

The DNA of your brand and your team is based on three 3 ingredients:

1. **Clarity**
   A clear alignment is built around three key aspects:

   a. Vision: What long-term future do we see for our network?

b. Mission: Why do we exist?
c. Core values: What guides our decisions and inspires our actions?

Here's a case in point: *Help Me*[2] is a franchisor of home care services for seniors.

Here's how we managed to create the network's alignment:

Our vision
Together, driven by a burning passion and unwavering commitment, we are building a bright future where every senior and person with diminishing autonomy in our local communities benefits from exceptional home care, enabling them to live as long as possible in their home environment.

Our mission and our purpose
Every day, we work with empathy to enable seniors to live with dignity in their own homes.

Our core values
Here's how we define respect, one of our core values:

At *Help Me*, we create a positive impact through our decisions and behaviors. By adopting a respectful, empathetic, and open-minded approach, we fully understand our customers' needs and offer them customized solutions.

---

[2] Fictitious name due to competitive issues

The main advantage for franchise network leaders to define a clear alignment is that it makes it easier to mobilize all team members. At *Help Me*, the proposed alignment has created new enthusiasm among both staff and stakeholders. It has also led to the successful recruitment of new franchisees by emphasizing differentiation in a sector. Differentiating the franchise necessarily involves the people who provide the service.

Clarity gives you power. Defining a clear alignment within your organization gives you the power to point the way forward and demand satisfactory performance from your network members.

Not doing so means you are **VOLUNTARILY** increasing the risk of weakening your growth.

a.   Without clear alignment, the choice of new franchisees depends too much on the size of the bank account, rather than on their real ability to succeed.

b.   Without clear alignment, your team members convey confusing and contradictory messages to franchisees.

c.   Without clear alignment, tolerance for non-performance is very high. The "never mind" attitude is omnipresent.

2.   **Demonstrate character**
One thing distinguishes outstanding franchisor team members: they have character. These leaders think, decide, and act with integrity. And, as you'd expect, they generally grow faster than their respective markets.

Why is having character so important?

Character means self-confidence, which is crucial to achieving and maintaining growth.

Although character development is first and foremost an individual choice and journey, franchise leaders can introduce into their network's culture five practices that foster a team's character:

Be honorable: Keep your promises and consider every word given as a valuable commitment.

Consistency and integrity: Ensure consistency in your actions and frequently evaluate your decisions to ensure they are in line with your values.

Proactive empathy: Tackle tough conversations with a deep understanding, revealing the strength of your character.

Humility and benevolence: Practice kindness with conviction and show humility with every success.

Proactivity: When faced with a challenge, commit yourself with determination and value every action and every relationship.

The key to success is character: **everyone** needs to demonstrate it, from success coaches (supervisors, franchise advisors) to senior managers and franchisees.

"Running a franchise network without a moral compass means dragging franchisees and your team into chaos."

— S. Breault

3. **The personal growth of your franchisees fosters your network's growth**
   A network without growth is a network that is failing.
   It's imperative for network leaders to avoid sabotaging growth by fostering a mindset of permanent growth.

   Yes, but...

   I believe that the most important yet neglected area of growth for franchise leaders is the personal growth of each franchisee. **Yes, you read that right, personal growth!**

   It will help all network leaders, including your franchisees, develop character.

   It will translate into personal initiatives on the part of both franchisees and franchisors to develop their skills, business practices, and new points of view.

   The franchisor must enable franchisees to broaden their horizons and become successful CEOs. Because a CEO isn't just about numbers; they are also, and above all, a leader with a vision. This is the only way I know of to avoid sabotaging the network's natural growth potential by the "good enough" syndrome that franchisees often experience (I'm "good enough," so why strive to grow?).

Ask yourself: with whom do you want to build a promising and prosperous future for your business?

I'm sure you already know the answer.

A common pitfall to avoid: complacency - The "good enough" *syndrome.*

Avoid falling into the trap of franchisors caught with characterless, unmotivated franchisees who sabotage growth—either because they're in the wrong place or because they're content to be "good enough."

There's nothing more frustrating and worrying than having franchisees in front of you who no longer believe, have a franchise location for sale, expect you to do the work for them, or are so satisfied with their situation that they no longer care about growth. This type of attitude is simply catastrophic for the organization's performance. Turning things around requires a superhuman effort because resistance to change and apathy have become encrusted in the franchisee's mindset.

Don't look for the culprit: it's you. As a leader, you are entirely responsible for your results. The solution to this impasse lies not only in the system I propose in this book but also in your commitment to becoming a growth leader.

Personal note:

This happened to me when I took over the presidency of a well-established franchise network in my region. I wouldn't wish it on anyone to have to turn around a franchise network populated, on the one hand, by disillusioned, apathetic franchisees with a single objective: to sell to the highest bidder and, on the other, by complacent "good enough" franchisees who stifle growth. What's more, the latter was holding the good franchisees hostage, as they were demanding change in order to continue. Phew! These were extremely difficult years. To turn things around, I had to change key members of the management team so that we could establish a new vision and mission that made sense as well as values that conveyed excellence and collaboration. Subsequently, we had to let go of several franchisees and refocus the network on a more modest base. All in all, those who stayed and the new ones who joined us shared the same values. To be honest, if I had it to do over again, I'd take even more time and effort to create and implement a clear alignment. Indeed, although we've made great strides, I wasn't able to create the common DNA that would foster a culture of excellence as I wanted, and the network suffered as a result. It was this experience, among others, that enabled me to develop the Franchisexcel© system I recommend in this book.

Master Assertive Communication to Transform Your Results and Boost Growth

Often, poor communication is blamed for lack of performance, failure, or conflict between franchisors and franchisees. This is a reality that can be changed. On closer examination, these failures are often due to one party trying to win over the other. Let's face it, this is counter-productive when you're aiming for a long-term partnership.

For you, franchise leaders, the solution is assertive communication. You're probably thinking that this is magical thinking and that it's impossible to implement when people don't get along and our objectives are misaligned.

What if it were all a lie?

Let me explain. Disagreements, differences of opinion, under-performance, and misunderstandings are inevitable in a franchisor-franchisee relationship. It's perfectly normal—and often even healthy. Conflicts allow us to clarify the state of the partnership and make decisions that benefit both parties.

However, these can spiral out of control, leading to turbulence within the network and a negative impact on growth and profitability. How many stories of lawsuits or the creation of franchisee associations have arisen because leaders didn't know how to communicate properly? The solution: communicate assertively, with the aim of finding solutions, rather than creating conflict.

Naturally, this works best if communication is already open and well-established to foster mutual trust. If not, it can be a real challenge!

What is assertive communication?

Assertive communication is the art of conveying your message frankly, directly, and respectfully, without falling into the traps of aggressiveness or passivity. Assertive communication, rooted in pre-established trust, guarantees fruitful collaboration and accelerated growth.

The "assertiveness triad" for effective communication

The relationship with franchisees is more fragile than it seems. It's very easy to use the power that comes automatically with the franchise agreement. But the mutual growth pact you have with your franchisees deserves much better. By using the "assertiveness triad," you can avoid many conflicts. Naturally, it's a good idea to train your franchisees in assertive communication so that everyone speaks the same language and uses the same communication approach.

> **Your attitude is your spokesperson:** More than your words, it's your behavior that defines the tone of a discussion. Treat your franchisees with respect. Keep in mind they are long-term partners. Encourage open discussion, and treat people with the consideration they deserve. Integrity, maturity, and generosity should be the cornerstones of your interactions.

Minimize the barriers to communication: Prejudice, distraction, selective listening, hasty thinking, or an unsuitable environment can muddy the message. Keep your mind focused and anchored on the essential facts. This is definitely a challenge for success coaches, as they are in regular contact with franchisees.

Listen with a clear purpose: Active listening is an art in itself. Put your interlocutor at ease, show empathy, and demonstrate patience. Never forget that a message needs to be repeated seven times to be understood. Ask open-ended questions guided by the 5 Ws[3] and make sure you capture the essence of the message. Before you judge or argue, make sure you know the facts.

When can you tell that assertive communication is lacking?

- Messages are not clear. As a result, there are more conflicts, or more time wasted re-explaining in order to explain.
- Tension is created because people don't know where they stand. This fosters insecurity, which prevents trust from taking root.
- You spend your time implementing controls and always have to "push" onto your franchisees. A lack of assertive communication is costly because the lack of trust doesn't allow for growth and forces you to spend more on control measures.

In a nutshell: gone are the days when communication within a franchise network was simply the transmission of information.

---

[3] *Why, What, When, How, How much*

In the modern, complex world of franchising, assertive communication has become a crucial skill for navigating the sometimes-tumultuous waters of business relationships. **It is a strategic lever for optimal results and sustained growth.**

Coach's Thoughts

I insist on the importance of the team, both that of the head office and that of the franchisees. In my practice, I too often see management teams that are weak and dependent on the CEO, and franchisees who don't team up with the franchisor and achieve sub-par performance. It's your responsibility as a franchise leader to surround yourself with excellent people. Without them, you won't get very far. Before you begin your transformation, I suggest a reflection based on these questions.

Q1: What are the characteristics of your team?

- Franchisor
- Network

Q2: Is this the team you want? Why or why not?

Q3: If I had to do it all over again, who wouldn't be part of the team? Why?

Q4: If you had to do it all over again, what would you do differently?

Q5: What's stopping you from doing it now?

Chapter 3

Operational Excellence: A Neglected Growth Asset for Franchisors

According to PwC, the top 20% of companies in their sector **outperform their competitors by 13 times** in terms of profit margin and revenue growth. This exceptional performance is not due to a secret formula, but rather to interdependent adjustments to their business and operational models—and the technology that supports them.

In franchising, this is called operational excellence.

"We are what we do over and over again. Excellence is therefore not an act, but a habit."

– Aristotle

The need for daily excellence

Let's face it, customers have changed. They want more, and doing the ordinary well is no longer extraordinary. Choices are multiplying, and everything is just a click away. It's the same with franchisees: increasingly educated, they have high, often unrealistic, expectations, propelled by access to social media that glorifies the entrepreneurial adventure. As a franchisor, you're competing with a multitude of entrepreneurial solutions, not to mention numerous competitors, regional, national, and international franchisors.

The same logic of excellence applies as much to franchisees' profitability as to attracting competent, committed employees or developing a team that supports franchisees' success.

If you don't strive for excellence and tolerate what isn't done properly, you're dragging your network down, with one consequence: depriving yourself of your capacity for healthy, rapid growth.

> In franchising, there's no room for average franchisors!
> These simply don't succeed.

Excellence Doesn't Mean Perfection!

Keep in mind that excellence doesn't mean perfection. Fostering excellence in your network doesn't mean wanting perfection, but rather wanting to improve every day on one of the variables that have a real impact on growth.

But what is operational excellence for a franchisor?

If we take the analogy of a top-level sports team and transpose it to a franchisor and its franchisees, operational excellence might look something like this:

What creates a team that excels at its sport?
Translation: What creates an exceptional franchisor?

A management team and trainers to match.
Translation: A competent, trustworthy franchising team that is connected with the network.

A clear goal.
Translation: A clear vision, supported by precise objectives.

Financial resources.
Translation: A high-performance business model for both franchisee and franchisor.

A winning mindset.
Translation: An obsession with creating a growth mindset with both franchisees and the franchising team.

The ability to attract the best possible talent for each position.
Translation: A structured and efficient recruitment and selection system that prioritizes the franchisee's aptitude for success.

A good game strategy.
Translation: Operations that ensure excellence at all levels.

Field leadership from both the coaching team and the players.
Translation: Teamwork where everyone knows and applies their role competently.

Unwavering character.
Translation: You have to walk the talk.

Discipline
Translation: An auditing system geared to continuous improvement, recognized and shared by all, as well as rituals to encourage learning and improvement.

Creativity
Translation: The ability to innovate in order to improve the customer experience and stay relevant.

Solidarity
Translation: A culture that puts the good of the brand and the customer before those of the franchisee and franchisor. The famous "All for one and one for all" or the U.S. Marines' "Leave no one behind" could be translated as "Leave no customer behind."

Does this sound impossible? Don't see how you can make it happen? You're not alone!

Thanks to the system developed in Chapters 4 to 10, you'll see how to integrate excellence into your network.

Excellence Means Working Together

Excellence in franchising is a matter for the franchisor **AND** the franchisees. The best way to achieve it is to work together on **a daily basis.**

STOP! Let's stop everything for two seconds. It looks good on paper, but it's a real challenge!

I couldn't agree more. By definition, the franchisee and franchisor are not geared in the same way. The franchisee is short-term oriented with a tactical and operational focus (you've got to serve your customers, don't you?), while the franchisor is medium- and long-term oriented to ensure the network's longevity. So what can be done to reconcile these two horizons and work together productively? The answer:

1. Reinforce network values
2. Become a learning franchisor

1. **Reinforcing network values**
   Reinforcing corporate values within a franchise network is crucial to maintaining brand cohesion and identity, and enabling each franchisee to act in accordance with the franchisor's principles and expectations.

   How do you embed values in your network?

   a. *Establish your values from the outset*
      - Integrate corporate values into the franchisee selection process.

   b. *Provide in-depth training*
      - Ensure that every franchisee and their staff understand and embody the company's values through dedicated training programs.

c. *Implement continuous, transparent communication*
   - Establish open and regular communication channels between franchisor and franchisees to discuss company values.

d. *Show recognition and give rewards*
   - Implement a recognition and reward system for franchisees who exemplify and apply the company's values.

e. *Provide adequate support*
   - Provide franchisees with the tools and support they need to integrate the company's values into their daily lives.

f. *Organize events and meetings*
   - Set up meetings and events for franchisees focused on sharing best practices and reinforcing the company's values and culture.

g. *Give visibility to your values*
   - Make sure the company's values are visible and pervasive throughout the franchise network.

h. *Provide feedback and enable improvement*
   - Encourage feedback and be ready to evolve according to franchisees' needs and experiences.

i. *Embody leadership*
   - Ensure that your leadership team embodies the company's values and sets an example.

In a nutshell: consistency in communicating and embodying your shared company values is essential at all levels of your organization to reinforce corporate values within your franchise network. This will enable franchisees to act in line with your values, and also help build a strong, consistent, and respected brand.

2. Become a learning franchisor

a. What is a learning franchisor?

The "learning franchisor" concept embraces the idea that a franchisor, regardless of its size or success, is constantly learning and adapting. It is part of a philosophy in which knowledge is welcomed, evaluated, and applied to continually improve the organization, processes, and relationships within the franchise network.

Key characteristics of this franchisor:

- Boundless curiosity: They constantly look for ways to understand the internal and external dynamics that influence the network.
- Adaptability: They modify strategies and processes in line with franchisees' learning and from lots of their feedback and comments.
- Collaboration: They integrate the knowledge and experience of franchisees and staff into the brand's development.
- Long-term perspective: They aim for sustainable growth and development rather than short-term gains.

b. How do I become a learning franchisor?

1. *Cultivate a growth mindset for everyone involved*
   - Embrace change and see mistakes as learning opportunities.

2. *Establish a robust feedback system involving franchisees*
   - Understand the strengths and weaknesses of the network from the inside, and to benefit from the practical experience of franchisees, and reinforce their commitment.

3. *Invest in continuing education*
   - Ensure that the network is constantly updated with the latest skills and knowledge to build operational excellence.

4. *Encourage innovation*
   - Stay relevant and competitive in the marketplace.

5. *Prioritize data analysis*
   - Make decisions based on concrete, measurable information.

6. *Practice active listening*
   - Fully understand franchisees' needs, concerns, and aspirations.

7. *Create a learning culture*
   o Make learning and continuous improvement part of the company's DNA.

Becoming a learning franchisor requires realigning attitudes, structures, and practices to place learning and adaptation at the heart of business strategy. This approach enriches not only the franchisor but also the entire network, stimulating innovation, commitment, and the sustainable success of the franchise ecosystem.

Excellence = Value Creation for Franchisor AND Franchisees

As you know, the best way to create long-term value is through the success of your franchisees.

That's the **GUARANTEE** of growth you need. But success isn't just financial. Examples abound of successful franchise networks that have lost a great deal of value or disappeared because value creation stopped working. How many successful franchise networks have been plagued by endless legal problems or a fatal loss of market share because the wheel just wouldn't turn?

So what's the problem?

In franchising, value creation is too often summed up by money. That's too simplistic.

Franchise CEOs who adopt a purely financial approach sometimes overlook the importance of the intangible elements that contribute to franchisee success and satisfaction. It's true. A financially successful franchisee will generally be satisfied. But it doesn't stop there. Their well-being, commitment, and motivation are also closely linked to their perception of the value they receive from the network and its leaders.

Concretely, a franchise that offers ongoing support and training to its franchisees not only ensures that their skills and knowledge are up to date but also demonstrates a willingness to invest in their long-term success. These initiatives generate a sense of belonging and brand loyalty that goes far beyond mere financial profitability.

Concretely, a franchisor who communicates assertively about opportunities and challenges, and provides franchisees with concrete, supportive tools, fosters a solid partnership and creates the groundwork for mutual prosperity. Value is created through financial success, but also through a strong network, supported by robust relationships and fruitful exchanges between franchisees and franchisors.

Concretely, franchisees are the first point of contact with customers. They represent YOUR brand locally. Their satisfaction, commitment, and success are directly reflected in the network's customer experience, brand image, and financial performance. Therefore, while financial success is essential, it's not the only variable determining the creation of value for the franchisee.

And you, as a franchisor, how can you develop your value?

Measuring a franchisor's value creation requires a multidimensional approach. It must take into account both intrinsic and extrinsic elements in order to assess not only the financial performance but also the sustainable development of the franchise network.

Here's the dashboard to focus on:

1. *Financial performance*
   o Sales growth overall and at individual franchise level
   o Profitability (franchisor/franchisees)
   o Network expansion

2. *Franchisee satisfaction and retention*
   o Retention rate
   o Satisfaction surveys
   o Testimonials and references

3. *Brand vitality*
   o Awareness
   o Customer appreciation
   o Customer loyalty
   o Marketing and advertising effectiveness

4. *Innovation and adaptation*
   o Constant innovation
   o Flexibility to adapt to the market
   o Technological proactivity

5. *Corporate culture and leadership*
   o Employee and franchisee commitment
   o Skills development
   o Adherence to corporate values

6. *Compliance and quality*
   - Compliance with standards
   - Audits

7. *Corporate Social Responsibility (CSR)*
   - Green initiatives
   - Community involvement

To make sure we're clear:

No operational excellence = No long-term profit
No operational excellence = Anemic growth or decline
No operational excellence = Under-performing franchisees
No operational excellence = Brand destruction

It's your thought leadership that makes operational excellence happen. It's not magic—it's hard work. But the reward is worth it!

Coach's Thoughts

As a franchise leader, have you ever considered the profound impact of operational excellence? Here are some thought-provoking questions to get you thinking:

Q1: How can operational excellence contribute to sustainable growth in your franchise network?

Q2: Are your franchisees prepared for success thanks to a culture of operational excellence?

Q3: What role does customer satisfaction play in your franchise's reputation, and how does operational excellence influence it?

Q4: Have you assessed the risks that operational excellence can help mitigate within your franchise system?

Q5: In a competitive market, how does operational excellence position your franchise for success and differentiation?

Reflecting on these questions can help you highlight the significant benefits that a commitment to operational excellence will bring to your franchise.

Part 2

Building Your Growth Leadership System

Chapter 4

The V.U.C.A. Challenge

We live in a V.U.C.A. (Volatile, Uncertain, Complex, and Ambiguous) world.

Volatile: Constant change forces us to adjust our plans. This instability brings uncertainty to decisions, whereas *franchisees seek stability and security.*

Uncertain: Predicting the future is becoming increasingly difficult. Once-stable variables are now unpredictable, requiring rapid adaptation of business models. *Franchisees, on the other hand, aspire to predictability.*

Complex: The stakes are multiplying, especially with the impact of technology on consumers, employees, operations, and franchisee recruitment. This complexity demands new skills and brings challenges, while *franchisees want operational simplicity.*

Ambiguous: Clear distinctions are disappearing in the face of globalization and digitalization. Guidelines are becoming blurred both in terms of societal values and government intervention.

Franchisees, for their part, are looking for precise guidelines and clear answers.

It's easy to see that the V.U.C.A. world we live in is a game-changer, but what can you do about it?

This is where Franchisexcel© really becomes important for you. Here's why.

- It's clear that if you want your network to grow successfully, your actions will make THE difference because they provide the energy needed to mobilize your franchise partners. Franchisexcel© enables you to organize and, above all, implement your strategy through your leadership actions. This system focuses on the power of individuals to achieve great things.

  Neglecting to implement Franchisexcel© exposes you to the risks we all know too well:

  - Little, inconsistent, or no growth
  - Poor quality of franchisees
  - Operational discrepancies
  - Lower customer loyalty as the network grows
  - Uncontrolled turnover of franchisees
  - No value creation
  - Conflicts within the network
  - Inability to attract and retain franchisor team members

Understanding Franchisexcel©

It's the results that count, right? You're just as right as your franchisees: you all want results. But results don't just happen. They depend on your leadership.

But...

When it comes to leadership development, most business leaders agree that it's a long and tedious road and that it's difficult to measure results. ROI can be very abstract. However, Franchisexcel© is an action-oriented system that encourages the emergence of leadership and produces results—not abstract concepts.

Outcomes are just ideas. Actions are results.

So your success as a franchise network leader depends much more on your actions than your ideas...

Why?

It's simple: your business partners have high expectations and are focused on results because their primary role is to act, not to create.

That's not to say that ideas aren't necessary, but they need to be turned into action to create tangible results. So, how do we get there?

The leadership model behind the Franchisexcel© system

My vision of franchising is simple. I'm firmly convinced that there are three key dimensions that make or break franchise networks.

1. The franchising competence of the network leaders
2. The connection between franchisor leaders and franchisees
3. Mutual trust within the network

These three dimensions form the basis of your leadership: it's the secret recipe! To achieve the results you want, you need to expand the area of common intersection through your actions in each sphere.

LESS PERFORMANT NETWORK

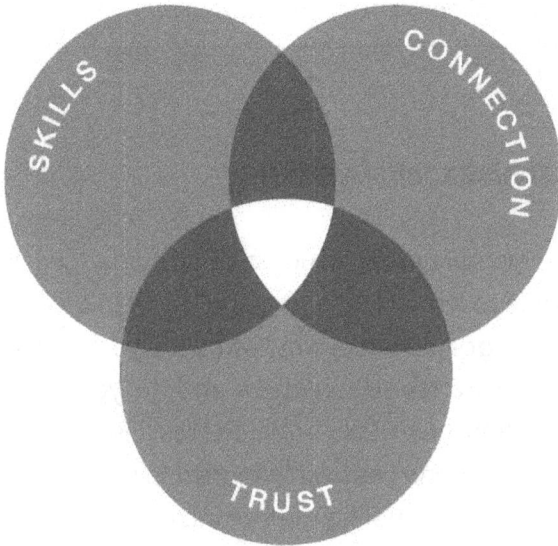

HIGH-PERFORMANCE NETWORK

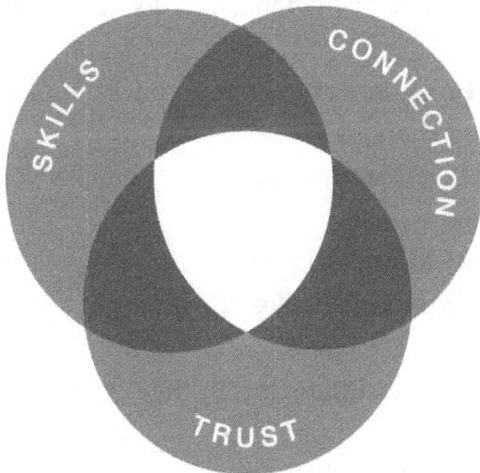

THE IMAGINE FRANCHISE GROWTH LEADERSHIP MODEL

> **Note:** Chapter 5: **Assess Your Franchise Leadership with Franchise Performance 360©** will help you understand how to use the three dimensions to your advantage.

The Franchisexcel© System

Franchise networks often struggle to leverage their full growth potential due to the lack of a genuine leadership system geared towards this goal. That's why, with 25 years of leadership experience in franchise networks and 15 years in executive coaching for franchise CEOs, I created Franchisexcel©. This system works in six stages and has been designed to stimulate exponential growth, tripling, quintupling or even increasing tenfold results in three to five years. This system puts people first, which is essential to organic growth and network expansion.

Franchisexcel© is tailor-made for you. Its main advantages are:

- **Clarity of action:** Guides you in implementing the desired changes
- **Structured leadership:** Clearly defines your actions as a leader
- **Prioritization:** Helps you determine your priorities
- **Team building:** Clarifies the profile of the team you want to build
- **Business discipline:** Instills the rigor needed to achieve your goals
- **Accountability:** Encourages commitment to results, both within your team and among your franchisees

- **Self-evaluation:** Allows you to assess your performance as a franchisor
- **Agility:** Facilitates adaptation to planned changes
- **Unity:** Ensures that all stakeholders share the same objectives

In a V.U.C.A. context where margins for error are shrinking, it's crucial to act quickly to build successful franchise networks. Franchisexcel© is the key to achieving this.

FRANCHISEXCEL©

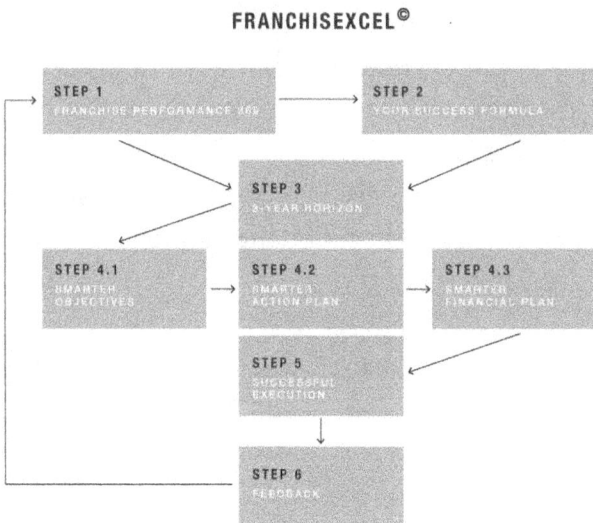

In a nutshell: The Franchisexcel© system is designed for franchise leaders looking to radically transform their network. By integrating these six steps into your leadership practice, you're not just leading a network: you're creating a movement toward sustainable success, based on an intentional growth leadership culture that is focused on excellence and built on trust.

It's YOUR Intention to Foster Excellence That Makes the Difference

Think about it for a moment. How many of your ambitious projects have ended in mixed success? How many times have you deviated from your initial trajectory, abandoning your objectives along the way? What do your franchisees think of these repeated failures? How does this affect your leadership of your team and franchisees? What opportunities have you missed? How much revenue has been lost due to a lack of clarity and determination in your plans?

Before plunging into Franchisexcel©, a few words of caution are in order. It's your intention to foster excellence that will make a difference. I know, I already introduced the notion of excellence in Chapter 3, but I insist on this point because it is not only critical. It will become your most important differentiator in order to create or rejuvenate your growth.

Your intention to create excellence is not just a practice, but a culture that you must embody and transmit throughout your journey in the Franchisexcel© system.

What does this mean?

Intentional excellence is the result of deliberate action, assertive communication, and constant alignment with a strong, well-articulated vision. Believe me, it's a real challenge to maintain this excellence; you'll need more courage and perseverance than you think. It will be more time-consuming, uncertain, and frustrating than you can imagine. However, it's worth the effort, because it's all about creating maximum value for your network. Your dream can finally come true!

"Excellence is never an accident. It's always the result of strong intention, sincere effort, and intelligent execution."

— Aristotle

The world is changing, customers are evolving, and their expectations are growing. Ordinary is no longer enough: excellence must become the norm.

Franchisees, too, are more informed and demanding than ever. Faced with increasing competition and a multitude of business options, you can no longer be satisfied with being an average franchisor. Your survival and that of your network depend on it.

Intentionally choosing to cultivate excellence means choosing growth. Excellence creates positive momentum, motivating those involved to work as a team, to surpass themselves, and to naturally push aside those who don't adhere to these high standards.

In sum, embracing intentional excellence means embarking on a journey of continuous growth and improvement. It's accepting the challenge of transforming not only your network but also every individual within it. It's an investment in the future as well as a promise of shared prosperity and lasting success.

Coach's Thoughts

At this point, perhaps you feel like dropping everything and carrying on as before. Change can bring its share of stress, but it pays off if you see it through. Getting an executive coach to accompany you may be an excellent decision.

Chapter 5

Assess Your Franchise Leadership with Franchise Performance 360©

The Imperative Foundations to Effectively Plan for Franchise Growth

The first step of the Franchisexcel© system is to conduct an assessment using Franchise Performance 360©. This step is mandatory because approaching a growth plan without adequate preparation is like navigating a storm without a compass. The consequences of this lack of preparation can be devastating for your franchise network. It can result in an inability to develop new franchises, a decrease in sales in your existing franchises, increased expenses to compensate for quality issues, etc. All of these scenarios can lead to a significant dent in your profits.

But the consequences don't stop there. Improvisation can lead to complex and costly legal problems, not to mention potential damage to your brand. Every impulsive decision or unstructured plan can severely impact your brand image and reputation, two invaluable assets in the world of franchising.

Ultimately, this lack of preparation and strategic vision not only harms your company, it also affects the prosperity of your franchisees. In other words, the entire network pays the price for this leadership failure. This is surely not the outcome you envision for your business and your partners.

With Franchise Performance 360©, you will be able to identify your main shortcomings. You will develop a targeted action plan to rectify them and capitalize on your strengths to increase your impact. Remember this maxim from Seth Godin, "Everything that is measured improves." By evaluating and understanding your weaknesses, you can transform them into growth opportunities.

Section 1: The Fundamental Qualities of Your Franchise

In my practice, I too often see franchisors who do not master the basics of business success in franchising. The consequences of this lack are multiple, but the most important thing is that franchisors and franchisees do not make the profits they should. Here is a comparison scale for franchisors published by the Franchise Performance Group (USA). It should guide you in your business.

Franchise life cycle	Number of new franchises per year	Target EBITDA
Start-up	0 to 5	-25% to + 5%
Emergence	5 to 15	-10% to +10%
Strong growth	15 to...	+10 to + 20%
Maturity		20% +

Source: Franchise Performance Group (USA)

Are your KPIs not up to the standards? Part of the answer is certainly in the lack of quality of the fundamental aspects of your business.

In addition to industry-specific factors, here are the main essential aspects of a successful franchise network:

- The strength of your strategy
- The quality of your team and organizational structure
- The alignment of your team members with your values
- The performance and robustness of your systems
- The practice of operational excellence within the network
- Your profitability as a franchisor
- The profitability of your franchisees
- The quality and relevance of your branding and marketing
- The brand value to your customers
- The brand value to potential franchisees

I believe that success in franchising is 50% the business dimension and 50% the human factor.

The first half of the assessment validates the business dimension of your franchise. Neglecting it exponentially increases the risk of failure.

The other 50% validates the growth leadership model. Skills-Connection-Trust = Success.

Tackling your growth is no small feat, and it is through your leadership that this can be done. The following sections will probably be real challenges for you. They call for a series of behaviors that, once realized, demonstrate your leadership to your team and franchisees and produce the results you want.

Section 2: Franchise Performance 360©

Beyond the bottom line, do you know what strategic aspect really determines your success?

> Is it your brand image? No.
>
> Innovation? No.
>
> Your advertising campaigns? Still no.

I believe the answer is the quality of your leadership with your franchisees. This should come as no surprise to you, but let me tell you that the best way to exercise that leadership is through action, not rhetoric. The second part of Franchise Performance 360© focuses on the effective leadership behaviors that drive your franchisees to align with your vision and stimulate the growth you desire.

Based on the "Skills-Connection-Trust = Success" model, this section of the assessment promises to trigger enriching discussions within your team.

Franchising Expertise

KKah's famous quote, *"Ambition without skills is a crime,"* underlines the crucial importance of competence in franchising. It's not just a requirement: it's a necessity at all organizational levels to create a leadership culture focused on excellence and growth. It's the key ingredient in a winning formula.

Why is your franchising expertise essential for franchisees?

Let's face it, the franchisee is looking for more than just a financial return. They are partnering with you to realize their entrepreneurial dream. If you could read their mind, here's what you'd get:

> "As a franchisee, *I have confidence in your skills to make my dream of being in business* with a *strong partner a reality.* I'll be able to put my *talents* to use and quickly make a *very good living from my franchise. This will enable me to* realize my *personal and family goals* and get a *return on my investment* faster than if I had started an independent business."

So, your franchising expertise has a direct impact on the franchisee's success.

The 3 key skills

In franchising, mistakes can have a disastrous multiplier effect. A network can falter and collapse under the weight of these mistakes. To avoid this, the franchisor must master three essential skills:

1. Master growth
2. Ensure operational excellence from top to bottom
3. Be obsessed with ROI

1. **Master growth**

   The growth of a franchise network depends first and foremost on all team members having a thorough understanding of the franchisee's business model, so as to be able to influence profitability through the decisions that affect it. Poorly thought-out promotions, sourcing errors, inefficient operating methods, and a lack of technology are all examples that illustrate a lack of mastery of the business model.

   Some ideas on growth:

   a. Organic growth

      Organic growth is the TRUE sign of a healthy network because flat or declining sales indicate a significant weakness in leadership. At this level, the easy excuse of, "What do you expect, it's the market" is not the answer franchisees are looking for.

   b. Growth through new franchises

      No franchisor can claim to maximize value creation without new franchises. It also depends on an effective recruitment and selection process—and the successful integration of newcomers. The development of franchisees' management skills is also crucial.

2. **Ensure operational excellence from top to bottom**

   Building a culture of operational excellence requires rigor and discipline. It must be anchored in the franchisor's vision and adopted at every level of the network.

What do we mean by operational excellence?

Let's use the metaphor of a Formula 1 team to illustrate.

The driver (franchisee) can't win alone. He needs a team.

The team (the franchisor) provides the best possible conditions for the driver to perform at their best.

Operational excellence is the execution of the winning race plan.

It's the shared hard work, lap after lap, that leads to victory.

That's what operational excellence is all about, for every customer who adopts your product or service.

It's a real challenge, but it's what separates ordinary franchisors who just get by from exceptional franchisors who develop full economic and human value and realize their dreams.

Watch out for weak links!

The success of a strategy lies in its execution, at every level.

"Good tactics can save even the worst strategy. Bad tactics can destroy even the best strategy."

— General Patton

However, I find that most franchisors have two weak links in their networks. By strengthening them, you'll give yourself the best chance of achieving success with a robust strategy.

a. The franchisee success coach
b. The complacent franchisee

Want to know more and find solutions? Check out Appendices D and E in the bonus pack you can receive by using the QR code on page 6.

3. **Be obsessed with ROI**
I believe that **the franchisor has everything to do with a franchisee's profitability.** Let me explain. A competent franchisor has monthly visibility of the profitability of each of their franchisees. They put mechanisms in place to share this information transparently with all franchisees in the network via common KPIs. This enables all franchisees to compare their performance and work together to find solutions to any discrepancies. What's more, the franchisor acts **immediately** on any lack of profitability on the part of their franchisees.

Why am I saying this?

80% of franchisors in America are small service businesses with limited resources and revenues of just a few million dollars. If franchisee profitability isn't a top priority for them, they're putting their profitability at risk.

Why should you be obsessed with ROI?

Because:

Generating a superior ROI is one of the reasons why the franchisee justifies all the costs (royalties and others) and investments required.

A superior ROI enables the franchisor to accelerate the changes needed to adjust to the market and protect the franchisee's future profitability.

A superior ROI is a magnet for new franchisees. It increases your ability to generate growth and offer solutions for franchisee succession.

Being ROI obsessed is not only necessary but mandatory for any franchisor who wants to succeed in this V.U.C.A. world.

This skill is often underdeveloped among the franchisor's operations staff. Yet it is an intrinsic part of the operations role. A well-informed franchisor will check the financial competence of team members.

Trust

- Why does a franchisee commit completely to the relationship with their franchisor?
- What motivates them to grow their business and become a multi-unit franchisee?
- What are the causes of deviant behavior in a franchisee?

- What are the causes of a franchisee's disengagement from a franchisor's strategic initiatives?
- What causes high turnover among franchisees?

Money, you may say! But that's only part of the equation. What triggers behavior is rarely rational, but rather emotional.

In my observations, the most profitable, best-performing, and committed franchisees trust the franchisor above all else, and whenever trust is lacking, problems pile up.

A **lack of trust is the greatest hidden expense for franchisors.** How many sales are lost because confidence is missing? How many necessary changes are delayed or abandoned because trust isn't strong enough to support them? How much energy is wasted in endless debates and disagreements, all stemming from a lack of trust?

Trust isn't just a "nice-to-have" – it's the cornerstone of a thriving franchise network. Without it, opportunities are missed, progress stalls, and relationships fracture. But with trust, everything changes. Collaboration flows naturally, decisions are made with confidence, and growth becomes inevitable.

The solution is clear: invest in trust, and you'll invest in the future success of your franchise.

What can be done to develop trust?

Let's understand that trust is, above all, a state of mind that translates into a multitude of behaviors which, if you adopt them, will positively affect the trust of your team members and franchisees. In franchising, trust doesn't come naturally. It has to be activated, reinforced, and shared before it can be established.

Trust is based on 5 elements:

1. Character
2. Commitment
3. Compassion
4. Consistency
5. Contribution

1. **Character:** (the mental and moral qualities of an individual). We could sum it all up in one sentence: think, decide, and act with integrity.

In contrast, a lack of character could be characterized by a lack of integrity, dishonesty, and laziness.

"To lead a franchise network without a moral compass is to lead franchisees and your team into chaos."

– S. Breault

How to do it?

The best way to demonstrate character is to make all decisions based on the organization's values.

2. **Commitment:** People trust people who keep their promises. There's really no compromise to be made with commitment because it's a vector for building trust.

"A franchisee's commitment is earned, not commanded".

– S. Breault

Within a franchise network, there's a lack of commitment when there's a lack of follow-through on projects presented and promises made, and a lack of loyalty to the franchise. Also, the "it's not my fault" syndrome is omnipresent. There is also a tolerance of non-performance by other network members, and a lack of decision-making.

How to do it?

The answer lies in assertiveness, discipline, and persistence. It's normal that not everyone is in tune with objectives, priorities, and the means to achieve them. It's the franchisor's role to ensure that the whole network is rowing in the same direction. Let's not forget that a message needs to be repeated at least seven times for it to be understood. Among my clients, I find that those who are most successful are fully and uncompromisingly committed to the success of the strategy we have co-created. There are no half-measures. They are assertive, disciplined, and very persistent.

3. **Compassion:** We trust people who put our interests before their own.
   How to do it?

   Within a franchise network, you have to learn to "catch" franchisees who are doing the right things, and recognize them in a specific, authentic, and personalized way.

4. **Consistency:** Consistency is the catalyst for trust. By being consistent, you create a domino effect. Everyone can rely on you, and by doing so, you foster trust.

   It's easy to see the lack of consistency in a network: it's chaos, work is irregular, the customer experience is highly variable from one franchise to the next, behavior is inconsistent, and there's a lot of unpredictability.

   What to do?

   My answer is simple. Create rituals. Rituals are part and parcel of a franchise network. They establish the security needed to build trust. Do you have rituals?

   For example:

   o Network-wide welcome celebrations for new franchise openings
   o Recognizing birthdays
   o Various regular meetings
   o Individual meetings (monthly, quarterly)

- ○ Annual one-on-one success planning meeting with each franchisee
- ○ Postcards to celebrate successes
- ○ Franchise visits
- ○ Annual convention
- ○ Etc.

5. **Contribution:** This is the ability to deliver the promised results. This is where all the other keys take shape, because it's all very well to have character and commitment, but if it doesn't deliver, what's the point?

There's no contribution when you have to sound the alarm everywhere, when disorganization reigns, when meetings are never-ending, when there's no follow-up, and so on.

Contribution is not a one-way street. Too often, I see franchisors organizing activities and launching programs to achieve results, without franchisees getting on board. Partnership is a two-way street, and franchisees are also expected to deliver results, because they have to contribute to the success of the team and the brand. That's the essence of partnership, isn't it?

"Together, we can achieve our goals and reach our dreams." That should be your motto.

So, choosing to develop trust is a strong leadership gesture. It's demanding and involves risks, but it helps forge a high-performance network.

Connection

The connection between franchisees and you, your employees, and your customers, is the cornerstone on which the positive impact of growth leadership is built.

Connection is the team spirit that permeates a network.

Team spirit is a sense of pride, camaraderie, and loyalty shared by the members of a particular group.

It's up to you to establish and nurture it. Without these connections, there's no commitment.

"People don't buy what you do, they buy why you do it. And what you do simply proves what you believe."

— S. Sinek

Three essential qualities for making connections

1. **Clarity**

   Clarity means conveying information accurately, understanding what is essential, and knowing what is necessary. It eliminates grey areas, providing the tools to move forward with confidence.

   Easier said than done, this leadership function is more than necessary. Franchisors often skip it entirely. With clarity, your message will be better understood, and you'll be able to progress more easily.

What to do?

Chapter 6, **Formulate Your Formula for Success**, offers solutions.

2. **Assertive communication**

   Poor communication is often blamed for failures and conflicts between franchisors and franchisees. These failures are often due to one party trying to win over the other. Let's face it, this is counter-productive when you're aiming for a long-term partnership.

   The solution is assertive communication. In a franchisor/franchisee relationship, disagreements, differences of opinion, misunderstandings, and potential conflicts are bound to arise. This is perfectly normal, and often healthy, as it enables the state of the partnership to be clarified, and mutually beneficial decisions to be made.

   Definition: Assertive communication is a way of expressing your point of view clearly and directly, without being aggressive or passive.

   By mastering the art of assertive communication, franchise leaders can avoid the conflicts and disagreements that are all too common in networks.

   Naturally, this works best if communication has been open and well-established beforehand, as it builds a foundation of mutual trust. Without it, it's a real challenge!

Assertive communication is therefore the most productive way to establish effective communication.

3. **Magnetism**

   By definition, a franchise network involves operational decentralization taken to the extreme. As a franchisor, you delegate the power to deliver your brand experience to customers to a third party: your franchisee. But what holds it all together?

   The franchise agreement and operating manual are only guides, but **they have no effect on the franchisee's intrinsic desire to do better**, to excel, to create an outstanding team, and to fully embrace the brand.

   So what does it take?

   Magnetism.

   Instead of apathetic franchisees who destroy the brand and don't like their franchise, I imagine you dream of having franchisees who are committed, enthusiastic about their projects, and invested in their work as much as in the development of the brand.

   Magnetism in a network is the franchisor's ability to attract and unite team members and franchisees to achieve the long-term goal in line with the network's values.

But what can you do to create this magnetism?

From what I've seen with my customers, what creates magnetism is **a combination of meaningful activities** aimed at developing a **sense of passion and pride** for the brand within the franchisor-franchisee team. This feeling cannot be bought with money. It's the magnetism that makes its members say they have the logo tattooed on their hearts.

Magnetism is not magic.

As the leader of your network, it's up to you to create it. To do this, don't hesitate to involve your team and franchisees. You'll come out a winner.

Finally, think of magnetism as the turbo-charged effect on all three components of the model. When people are attracted to leaders, buy-in is that much stronger.

Do you doubt the ROI impact of your connection investment?

This excerpt from John Maxwell's book *High Road Leadership: Bringing People Together in a World That Divides will convince you.*

Enjoy the Positive Return

"High-road leaders don't value people to get a reward. That's not the right motivation. However, there is

eventually a return for valuing people. It comes with time and consistency. I've found three kinds of returns you can receive by valuing others:

A Relational Return: When you value all people, you can't help but build better relationships. You open doors to new relationships with every interaction, and you improve relationships with individuals with whom you're already acquainted.

An Emotional Return: I've never known a person who values others and adds value to them not to receive an emotional return from doing it. Few things in life are more rewarding than helping another human being.

A Leadership Return: Valuing people also has a return for you as a leader. When you care about people, value them, and act in their best interest, your influence increases because they trust you and have a greater desire to work with you. And even if there isn't a direct connection with you on your team or in your organization, they will want to help you succeed or connect you to people who can help you directly."

Coach's Thoughts

How do we know if we are optimal in our skills and our ability to develop trust and connections as a franchisor?

You might say that results are what count, right? Well, no, results are just one of the variables to consider. To me, what's important is the sum of the proactive actions you take.

Here are some reflective questions to consider:

Q1: Can we improve our franchising skills? If so, which ones? What's the plan?

Q2: What score would you get if you conducted a franchisee satisfaction survey? Which aspects would be the strongest, and which the weakest?

Q3: Do we have leadership practices that build trust with our franchisees?

Q4: Do we have a strong "group morale" within our network? If yes, why? If not, why?

"Knowing others is intelligence. Knowing yourself is true wisdom."

– Lao Tzu

Formulate Your Formula for Success

Let's face it, success in franchising is demanding. However, I believe that we are fully responsible for the results we achieve. For a franchise leader, this necessarily means the success of the franchisees. Of course, you're not responsible for the individual success of each of your franchisees, but you are responsible for creating the conditions for them to succeed.

But what is success in franchising, and how can you create the conditions to help your team and franchisees get there?

This is where the following formula can help guide your actions.

% Faith x % Focus x % Effort = % Success

It's the combination of your actions on these three aspects that catalyzes **your franchise's success formula.**

The secret of the formula is the **multiplier effect.** To get compelling results, you have to put in the effort!

Without being a math whiz, you can see that 100% is virtually impossible to achieve. The idea here is that to have a **lasting impact** on franchisees, your actions must be significant.

An example to better understand the leverage effect of the formula

Imagine that, following your assessment in Franchise Performance 360©, you must put in place a four-step plan focusing on impactful actions that develop the Focus variable in the formula. Over time, your Focus results improve, and you can see the effect on your success percentage.

Step	Faith	Focus	Effort	Success
1	60%	50%	60%	18%
2	60%	75%	60%	27%
3	60%	85%	60%	31%
4	60%	100%	60%	36%

By doubling the Focus variable, you double your success rate.

Of course, you'll want to define more precisely what success is for you and your network. That's what we'd call your ultimate goal.

Want to know more and find solutions? Check for the bonus pack you can receive by using the QR code on page 6.

Let's explore each variable a little further.

% Faith

In the context of this book, faith does not refer to a religious belief, but to confidence in the success of your project. Franchisees associate themselves with your brand and system in an act of faith. So how do you cultivate this faith within a franchise network?

Faith is based on three inseparable aspects: mindset, skills, and reinforcement.

Mindset: Clarity is essential for a franchise leader to bring franchisees together. This includes defining a vision, a mission for customers and franchisees, clear values, mutual expectations, and an ultimate goal. These align all members of the network with the desired outcome.

Skills: Skills are crucial to building faith in success. The secret: develop a culture of continuous training in your network, covering knowledge, know-how, and, above all, the interpersonal skills of franchise leaders. Most franchisors are very good at working on the first two skills, but very few focus on the third: leadership skills. Yet this is fundamental to fostering the attitude of growth, commitment, and collaboration you're looking for.

Reinforcement: Regular, organized rituals help maintain and develop faith. Creating a culture where being a team member is a privilege, and a source of pride reinforces group morale and influence over franchisees.

The ZZZ case study.[4] The inactive network:

---

4   For confidentiality reasons, I cannot give the name of this franchisor.

Founded by 14 franchisees ten years ago following the bankruptcy of the franchisor, this network has built up a good reputation over the years in the market it serves. Since the end of COVID-19, the growth of the network has stalled, franchisee performance has stagnated or deteriorated, and operational excellence has been achieved by a few individuals through their individual efforts. The market is changing rapidly, and the network has no plan to adapt, regain, or conquer market share. Leadership is small-minded, focusing exclusively on marketing.

In the course of my work, and after the shock of the Franchise Performance 360© results, it became clear that this franchisor's success formula simply didn't exist.

Following the success formula creation exercise, all but one franchisee signed up for a highly ambitious three-year transformation plan to achieve 10X growth and value creation over five years.

The key element in this new formula was Faith. Indeed, all franchisees decided to commit and invest directly in the franchisor through the acquisition of shares. They wanted to completely change the franchise business model to enable the franchisor, of which they are shareholders, to have the means to achieve the vision.

Overnight, despite the insecurity associated with change, meetings became dynamic, strategic initiatives were implemented one by one with discipline and rigor, and performance levels improved.

It's still too early to measure the impact on value creation, but performance and franchisee commitment to the plan suggest that this network is on the right track.

In sum, the faith you can transmit to everyone is a strategic asset for your success. It is built through a clear vision, skills development, and constant reinforcement.

% Focus

As you already know, to increase your chances of success in franchising, you need to stay on course and focus on the essentials. It doesn't matter whether you're an emerging, fast-growing, or mature network. Granted, staying focused isn't always easy.

All too often, I meet franchisors who are busy being busy; they are only putting out fires they themselves have lit through lack of focus.

So what do you have to do to keep the focus?

I often quote this phrase to my clients, "It's urgent to do nothing. It's time to think."

What to think about? Here are four ways to think about it:

1. Stop believing you're a superhero
2. Ask yourself the right questions
3. Learn to prioritize
4. Be SMARTER

1. **Stop believing you're the superhero**
   As a leader, you're constantly in a hurry, with people lining up outside your office door to get answers. You end up not making decisions. You lack focus.

   Staying focused means making choices, saying no, and remaining patient. It also means learning to work with your team members so that they, too, put their shoulder to the wheel. As an entrepreneur, you always have a ton of good ideas for getting things done. But are they always the right things to do? At the right time? With the right resources?

2. **Ask yourself the right questions**
   Not sure if you're focused? These questions can help you see things more clearly:

   - Where are you headed?
   - Why are you going?
   - Are the steps to get there clear and measurable?
   - Who do you need to work with to get there?

   You'll find that this pause often clarifies things and, above all, puts the situation, your idea, or your project into perspective.

3. **Learn to prioritize**
   What a nightmare it is to have to prioritize! I imagine you think everything is important. Unfortunately, this is the reflex of most franchise leaders. You have to understand

that not prioritizing is what causes a lack of focus. It dilutes your efforts, and you don't achieve your goals.

The YC case study.[5]

In this franchise network, the most popular phrase among the leadership team was, "Yes, I'll take care of it." Despite this, nothing was happening, because all of the management team members were swamped dealing with problems that had become urgent because they hadn't been resolved at the right time. Most of these were problems that belonged to the franchisees. Interestingly, in the minds of the management team, it was imperative to compensate for the fact that franchisees were not adequately looking after their franchises.

As a result, the team was exhausted and didn't know what to do. The only preferred solution was to hire more staff. Inevitably, it was chaos for both franchisor and franchisees.

Right from the start of the exercise to create the success formula, the Focus variable was identified: the BIG problem was that leaders didn't know how to prioritize and delegate properly so as not to take on responsibilities that weren't their business. The first month the team applied the principles of prioritization and delegation. Guess what? A wave of fresh air permeated the organization. Franchisees said they were happier, as things were clearer for them.

---

[5] For confidentiality reasons, I cannot give the name of this franchisor.

We'll have to stay tuned as some franchise leaders go back to their old ways.

Focus doesn't just apply to day-to-day business. It also applies to strategic alignment. Indeed, franchisors with a clear strategic focus are the most successful. Too often, I meet franchisors who pursue too many markets or too many objectives at once. They lose focus on value creation.

4. **Be SMARTER**
    The solution to lack of focus lies in a clear strategy of objectives and a realistic plan for achieving them. The Franchisexcel© growth leadership system has been specially developed to avoid this situation. Chapter 8 details the crucial elements of being SMARTER.

    However, being SMARTER isn't just about goals. It means staying connected with franchisees to maximize the impact of decisions to create maximum value.

    Remember, focus enhances your performance as a leader.

% Effort

Effort in franchising refers not only to the culture of operational excellence but also to the importance of consistency. The problem with effort is that it's hard to maintain. To exert it consistently, it's easier to split it up. Some types of effort are easier than others.

For a franchise leader, there are four types of efforts to focus on:

1. **The Mindset**

   In my opinion, a growth mindset must be THE priority for you and each of your franchisees, because everyone has an obligation to grow if they want to continue to prosper. It's up to you to develop it, using your best people to lead by example. This state of mind is not easy to instill in everyone and requires constant work. Remember that tolerating a lack of performance discourages the best performers.

   That is why I adhere to the principle of "benevolent pruning" of low-performing franchisees (those who don't have a growth mindset). What I mean here is that the last option a franchisor should take is to ask a franchisee to leave the network using legal means. In my opinion and in my experience, it's possible to find mutually beneficial solutions in 90% of cases. It just takes courage and creativity on the part of the network's leaders.

   Want to know more and find solutions? Check out the Appendix in the bonus pack you can receive by using the QR code on page 6.

2. **Skills Development**

   In the V.U.C.A. world in which we live, constant skills development is a priority. As a franchisor, you need to invest time and resources in developing your own skills, and those of your franchisees. These efforts must focus on developing operational skills, know-how, and interpersonal skills (or the ability to be a successful leader). There are a multitude of ways to do this. But one thing is certain: it must be a regular, organized process. Thinking that you effectively train your franchisees once a year at the annual convention is an illusion. Don't forget that this investment also promotes your growth.

Here's a list of skills a franchisor should develop:

o Operational skills
o All elements specific to your operating system, marketing, management, and human resources, technology, etc.
o All the best practices for mastering skills:
  ▪ Developing franchisee leadership
  ▪ Self-leadership: Leading by example
  ▪ Managing priorities
  ▪ Mobilizing communication
  ▪ Efficient delegation
  ▪ Difficult conversations
  ▪ Building a team
  ▪ Team success
  ▪ Acting as a leader in the community and raising awareness about franchise
  ▪ And many others, as you might expect.

3. **Building Trust (see Chapter 5)**
   As you now know, trust plays a major role in both your growth and profitability. Think of this effort as an exercise in communicating better—to make yourself better understood by your network and franchisees. This way, you'll stop wasting time arguing endlessly, constantly being on the defensive to justify yourself to your

franchisees, and you'll be much more comfortable working with them to find real solutions and solve problems.

4. **Developing Connections (see Chapter 5)**
This is probably the effort you'll find least rewarding. Establishing connections with people requires little money, but a lot of time. Your best bet? Be proactive and create opportunities to connect with your franchisees.

In your mind, the % Effort component of the formula is probably the most demanding. And you're right, because it addresses the importance of people in your success as a franchisor. Effort is paramount to your success.

As a leader, remember this quote:

"In success, there is more courage than talent."

– F. Leclerc

Coach's Thoughts

With the formula for your success, you set the bar where you want it.

Keep in mind that it's your determination, coupled with that of your team and franchisees, that will propel your network forward.

Defining your formula for success is an exercise that requires you to take a step back.

Remember:

"Great things in business are never done by one person; they're done by a team of people."

– Steve Jobs

Want to know more and find solutions? Check for the bonus pack you can receive by using the QR code on page 6.

Chapter 7

Developing a Transformative Strategy

"Hope is not a strategy. Luck is not a parameter. Fear is not an option"

– J. Cameron

Growth doesn't happen by itself, and without your leadership, you won't be able to create all the wealth your franchise has to offer.

To achieve this, the recipe for success is the development of a strategy supported by a solid, well-thought-out plan. Normally, a strategy is drawn up with a three-year horizon and proposes the transformations needed to maintain or develop the desired performance.

Skeptical? Let's take a look at the main consequences of not having a strategy.

Lack of direction: Without a strategic plan, you're sailing without a compass, risking scattering your efforts and losing sight of your long-term goals.

Change management: The absence of a strategy leaves you vulnerable to market turbulence, limiting your ability to adapt quickly to new developments and business opportunities.

Franchisee cohesion: Without a clear objective, your network risks lacking unity and motivation, essential elements for harmonious, sustained growth.

Risky decision-making: Without planning, your decisions can become impulsive and haphazard, significantly increasing the risk of failure.

Operational inefficiency: Without a well-defined strategy, your resources could be misused, leading to inefficiency and unnecessary costs.

Growth problems: A network without a strategic plan struggles to develop in a structured way, hindering your expansion and success.

Reputation and brand image: Strategic confusion can erode your brand image, which is essential to attracting franchisees and customers.

Competition: Failing to anticipate your competitors' moves with a proactive strategy puts you in a weak position vis-à-vis them.

Don't risk being a franchisor without a strategic plan. You'd be like a rudderless ship, at the mercy of market waves and competitive winds.

Phase 1: Three-year Horizon

I recommend a strategic plan every three years. The reason is simple: V.U.C.A.

The method may seem simple, but it requires discipline and teamwork. Think of your strategy as the engine of your network.

Let's see what it's all about:

Step 1: Gather key information from your Franchise Performance 360© assessment. This assessment should be carried out as a team.

To make your planning more effective, I recommend that you carry out a confidential franchisee satisfaction survey during the year. The project can take three or four months to complete. With the results, you'll be able to better respond to your franchisees' issues, and not just your own, when it comes to strategic planning.

Step 2: Gather the findings of your work by filtering them through the three dimensions (Faith, Focus, Effort) of your franchise's success formula (Chapter 6). The idea here is to better identify the strategic objectives that have an impact on your growth leadership.

> **Note:** it may be relevant to include the results of market studies, a new geographical development plan, economic projection studies, trends, or direct or indirect competition, to avoid making blind decisions.

Coach's advice: Don't use the results of these studies to excuse your lack of ambition for growth. That would be a mistake. Indeed, if you or your franchisees don't grow, you're destroying your value. However, use the results of the studies to come up with ideas that will help you accelerate your growth.

Step 3: Visualize your company in three years time and define the strategic objectives you want to achieve.

The simplest way is to think in terms of business sectors with budgetary responsibilities.

The question: What will your network look like in three years time?

Here's an example to illustrate the formula of success.

For example, ABC e-foil is a new franchisor in the world of an up-and-coming water sport: e-foil electric surfing.

What's the success formula?

Faith: The entire network shares our vision, mission, and values

Our franchisees are passionate about the sport we offer, practicing it with fervor and acting as true ambassadors.

We create a worldwide community of fans of our new sport.

Our rituals for creating the culture we desire are practiced by all franchisees.

Focus: All our resources are used to maximize the value creation of our franchise

We aim to be the benchmark brand for upscale, aquatic vacation resorts in the USA, Mexico, the Caribbean, and South America.

We make sure that our franchisees are as competent as experts and offer a highly personalized quality of experience.

We work closely with our manufacturer to constantly improve the technology we use.

Effort: We focus on our strategic priorities

70% of the CEO's time is spent on growth.

We develop marketing programs that drive traffic to our franchisees.

We invest all our profits in growth.

The following sections are standard and do not require additional explanations.

General

What is your market positioning? What makes you different?

What sales will the network generate?

How many franchises will be in operation?

Who will be part of the franchisor's team?

What profits should we have? What should be the weighted profits of franchisees after three years of operation?

Business sectors

Development: Which markets will be covered?

Real estate/construction: What will be the state of our real estate pipeline?

Operations: What would best describe our operating culture?

Procurement: What's the best description of our procurement system?

Technology: What will be the state of our technology system?

Marketing: How will customers appreciate our brand?

Human resources: What will be the state of our human resources (franchisor and franchisees)

etc.?

Note: This list is not exhaustive and must be adapted to your network.

The idea here is to take a broad view and not get bogged down in operational details.

Each long-term objective needs to have a clearly identified person in charge who is capable of taking action.

> **Note:** the famous statement "it's everyone's responsibility" doesn't wash with me.

Also note: at this stage, you really need to distinguish between strategic objectives (what you want to achieve) and tactical objectives (how we're going to get there in the coming year).

Each question should have no more than three strategic objectives.

Once this step has been completed, you can move on to the SMARTER step (Chapter 8).

Why Don't Most Strategies Work?

"When you don't know where you're going, all roads lead nowhere."

– H. Kissinger

Most strategies fail for a number of common reasons. Here are some of the main factors:

1. **Insufficient data and analysis:** Developing a strategy without a thorough understanding of the market, the

competition, and your organization's internal capabilities can lead to unrealistic or ineffective plans. With **Franchise Performance 360©** (Chapter 5), you have an extremely effective tool at your disposal to help you get your bearings.

2. **Excessive complexity:** Overly complex strategies can be difficult to understand and implement. In straightforwardness, simplicity, and clarity are essential so that everyone involved can easily follow and execute the plan. The exercise of determining your formula for success (Chapter 6) is the cornerstone of this dimension.

3. **Lack of leadership and accountability:** Successful strategies require strong leadership and clear accountability. Without leaders capable of driving the strategy forward, and without individuals responsible for specific tasks, efforts can become unproductive. It's this factor that often fails my customers. And yet, this is where execution takes shape. All too often, the franchisor doesn't have the right resources to ensure that everything goes according to plan.

> ### The case of PP[6]: The network managed at the head office
>
> The following example highlights a situation I regularly see with franchisors: that of underestimating the need for resources to be able to implement the strategy.

---

[6] Fictitious name due to competition.

PP is an emerging franchisor in the home service sector. It has enjoyed interesting growth in the first two years of its franchise program. The leaders are also busy with two other companies in the same group. The original plan focused on recruiting new franchisees and providing initial technical training. The rest is "call me if you need anything," advertising, and supply management. As early as the second year, the leaders noticed that the franchisees' performance was lacking. What was bound to happen happened: 30% of the network disappeared in the third year, and a franchisee had committed fraud. So they had to start all over again, coming to the conclusion that without someone dedicated full-time to the success of the network, their efforts would be in vain.

This example shows that time and money are wasted through a lack of vision of a strategy's number 1 success factor: execution.

4. **Ignoring the human factor:** Strategies often focus on processes and results, but neglect the human element. Motivating, engaging, and training the franchisor's team and franchisees is crucial to the successful implementation of the strategy.

Given my background as a CEO and having worked as an executive coach with over 100 networks in 15 years, I find that this factor is the most poorly assessed by franchisors. One of the lessons I've learned from my experience is that franchisees' silence in the face of change doesn't mean they accept it.

In my opinion, the franchisor has a huge responsibility in getting the franchisee to commit to the strategy. He or she has to be convincing, but also know how to demonstrate the benefits of change. What's more, they must be able to listen to franchisees' grievances, which are often justified. Of course, I'm not talking here about complacent or under-performing franchisees, but about network leaders. In general, they have the solutions to bring about the changes that deserve to be promoted by the franchisor.

The same applies to the franchisor's team. How many times have I heard staff say things like, "I don't know why it's the way it is, but there's nothing I can do about it." Imagine the reaction of the franchisee who has to do everything possible.

Note: *There's a question that needs to be asked in the strategic planning exercise. Do you need to involve franchisees with you? In my opinion, yes. You need to find a way of doing this, for example by involving them in the reflection exercise following publication of the satisfaction survey results. The best thing to do is to set up a small committee to work on certain objectives that will form part of the strategy.*

You can also set up a franchisee advisory committee. It will deal with certain strategic issues and seek franchisees' opinions and comments. They often have realistic ideas for solutions.

Involving certain franchisees in the strategic planning process will help you increase buy-in from all franchisees since they will have been represented, and their ideas and suggestions will have been conveyed to the franchisor.

5. **Unrealistic expectations:** Setting goals that are too ambitious or deadlines that are too tight can lead to failure. It's important to set realistic expectations and allow sufficient time for the strategy to be achieved.

   Let me give you a personal example that I learned from.

   I accepted the position of president (it was my first role as a president) of a company specializing in electronic security for the residential, commercial, and institutional sectors. My initial mandate was to double sales in three years. Due to a lack of experience and performance anxiety, I threw myself headlong into drawing up a plan without doing a proper assessment (at the time, Franchise Performance 360© didn't exist ;-)) or involving the existing team, whom I didn't know very well. I relied on my instinct and what I saw. But the plan didn't work at all. Instead of achieving growth, I was forced to put the whole plan on hold. Indeed, after a few months, I had to face the facts: the company was in very bad shape. The management team didn't believe in it and didn't have the necessary skills. The operating system, finances, and general state of the network were also inadequate. In fact, the company had no capacity whatsoever to execute the plan. In short, it was a disaster, and my fault. As a result, I tried to turn things around for two years, but the board of directors decided I was no longer the right man for the job and fired me.

The lesson I've learned from this life-changing experience is that, without working on the human side, you'll never achieve your goals. Good execution can make up for bad strategy.

With all my clients, I dwell at length on the human factor during strategic planning. You need to ask yourself questions like:

- Do we have the right team?
- Is everyone (management team and franchisees) in the right place, sharing our values, with the right skills and abilities? Does everyone have the necessary drive to succeed?

Almost every time, we have to revise our objectives to give ourselves the means to execute the strategy.

My motto: *Less is more.*

About KPIs

Key Performance Indicators (KPIs) are derived from the development of strategic objectives (see Chapter 8). Establishing KPIs can be very useful. By creating a dashboard, they can help you make informed decisions about the results you're achieving. However, as the CEO of a network, you need to think strategically about your dashboard, and resist the traditional KPIs that are too often put in place and not really measured or monitored as they should be.

Let me explain:

As a network leader, the KPIs you follow must reflect the strategy you want. This strategy has taken shape in the development of your success formula. In my opinion, your dashboard should boil down to five elements and answer the following questions:

- Is our growth in line with our objectives?
- Is faith in our network at the level we want it to be?
- Are we (and our franchisees) 100% focused on executing our strategy?
- Is everyone making an effort, the right one?
- Does the network's financial performance (and our own) match our objectives?

By reflecting on these questions rather than taking disconnected actions, you'll gain a much clearer sense of how your strategy is progressing.

When I do the dashboard exercise with my clients, we develop the matrix and weigh each of the KPIs by sector to create a summary table for the CEO that answers the questions. Just as we do with **Franchise Performance 360©**.

Coach's Thoughts

The strategy should be seen as a tool for mobilizing all the forces in your network to achieve your objectives.

Make a clear distinction between the strategic plan, which is a roadmap for the future, and the budget. This will make it easier not to lose sight of your strategic objectives.

Take the time to mobilize everyone.

The best strategies fit on one page and are easily understood by everyone.

Want to know more and find solutions? Check the bonus pack you can receive by scanning the QR code on page 6.

Chapter 8

Get Smarter with SMARTER

I use the expression SMARTER to illustrate not only how to set goals, but also to mean that it's an exercise that requires a lot of *smartness* on your part and that of your management team. You'll have to take risks, make choices, say no, and postpone. Creating an action plan requires a great deal of judgment on your part.

There are three areas of *smartness* that, I believe, make for a successful action plan.

- The objectives
- The relevance of the plan
- The budget

SMARTER - The Objectives

SMARTER is an improved approach to goal setting. It ensures that objectives are clear and achievable, but also motivating and rewarding. The meaning of SMARTER is as follows:

Specific
Measurable
Achievable
Relevant
Timely
Evaluate
Readjust

Want to know more and find solutions? Check out the bonus pack you can receive by scanning the QR code on page 6.

The difference with the classic SMART method comes from the last two points: evaluating and readjusting. These last two factors make a huge difference in terms of adherence to the plan and the agility required to deal with unexpected events.

Setting goals is a difficult and frustrating exercise, but once you've established them, your action plan will make sense—and you'll find it easier to stay focused.

WARNING:
Goals are not a grocery list or simple tasks to be accomplished, but rather guidelines that prioritize choices, resources, and actions.

SMARTER - The Relevant Action Plan

An effective action plan in a franchise network is one that balances brand consistency with the individual needs of franchisees, while promoting the growth and success of the network as a whole. It's an exercise that looks at all sectors, and everyone should have one.

Here are a few questions to ask yourself to help you optimize your action plan.

- Are the objectives in line with the network's strategic goals?
- Is the plan written in such a way that everyone (including franchisees) understands it and sees what they have to do?
- Have you identified and taken steps to meet the training or support needs required to achieve the plan's objectives?
- Has standardization been taken into account? Have the means and resources to achieve this been identified?
- Have you identified how to measure the progress and performance of your initiatives using clear metrics and checkpoints?
- Are performance managers (typically, success coaches, supervisors, and franchise advisors) and franchisees able to achieve the objectives that belong to them?
- Do you have all the material and marketing (or other) resources in place to facilitate the execution of the plan?
- Does the plan include a feedback mechanism for franchisees?
- Have you identified potential obstacles and developed strategies to mitigate their impact?

Let's be clear:
For your franchisees, it's the action plan that counts, because they don't have much control over the strategy. They can, however, achieve convincing results if they have the faith, focus, and effort to make the action plan a success, since they can control many of these elements.

SMARTER - The Budget

I'm always amazed at the number of franchisors who don't have a budget and manage their business using only their bank account as an information tool.

Yet not having a budget has many consequences:

Lack of financial control: No monitoring or control over expenses and investments.

Planning difficulties: Future initiatives, expansion, franchisee recruitment, and system improvements.

Risk of insolvency: Risk of cash flow problems, leading to financial difficulties or even insolvency.

Loss of franchisee confidence: Franchisees expect the franchisor to manage the network professionally and responsibly.

Lack of investment in the network: Inability to invest in crucial areas such as R&D, training, and franchisee support.

Inability to react to market changes: No reserve for unforeseen situations or market opportunities.

Problems with investors and lenders: Investors and lenders may be reluctant to commit to a franchise network without solid, transparent financial management.

Difficulties in measuring performance: Without a budget, it's difficult to measure the success or failure of strategies and initiatives.

The budget is the franchise leader's working tool. It serves as a forecast but also establishes sound management and the delegation of responsibilities. It's a worthwhile investment to make.

Of course, a budget that is not rigorously implemented is worthless. My clients often tell me that by making a budget, they feel they won't be able to be opportunistic in the marketplace. FALSE: A budget makes it easier to assess your real ability to seize opportunities and reduce the risk of slippage.

Coach's Thoughts

Is this really necessary, you might ask?

I can hear you thinking:

"I don't have the time."
"It's useless, it won't have any effect on my network."
"It's complicated, my team doesn't have the skills."
"It's expensive."
"Why a plan when everything's going well?"
"Planning is not my forte."
"We can't predict the future, so why try to plan it?"
"Given the current situation, we need to focus on the short term."
"I want to keep all the flexibility."

Ask yourself:

If I offered you the chance to get on a sailboat and cross the Atlantic Ocean with a compass as your only navigation tool, without knowing whether you were properly equipped to make the crossing, would you jump in?

Think like a growth leader. Imagine the satisfaction of your franchisees when you present them with a well-developed, coherent action plan. Don't you think it would be easier, less costly, and, above all, more harmonious to adhere to your objectives?

Chapter 9

Beyond the Plan,
There Are the People

As you well know, your success depends on the success of your franchisees. This interdependence is the beauty and challenge of franchising. There's no point in going through the whole exercise if only to present it to the management team or shareholders. You need to engage franchisees in your new adventure.

Franchisors are too often poor salespeople for their initiatives.

Let me explain: most of my customers fail to sell their ideas, innovations, or new strategies properly. They take it for granted that their franchisees are "captive customers." But this is not true.

Your franchisees are like the cylinders in an engine: if one or more aren't working properly, your performance suffers. That's why I'm a firm believer in the importance of managing change in a humane but decisive way, with everyone on board.

You need to go beyond the tipping point to maximize the results of your strategy, and this starts well before Day 1.

Creating a wave of growth requires a major effort on your part. It must be made at the right time, with discipline and, above all, conviction.

Remember, you're not going to the championship after just one game of the season.

Three Principles Should Guide Your Efforts to Engage Franchisees

1. **Changes create chaos before they are mastered.**
   Fear: In franchising, every strategic plan involves changes that affect franchisees, whether they're new developments, investments, or abandonments. By recognizing that, for many of your franchisees, change will be a real challenge, you'll take the right steps to ease the transition.

   Never underestimate the unspoken needs of your franchise partners. They're often skeptical about change and won't say what they think, but silence doesn't mean yes. Forcing the issue will only alienate them even more.

   Active listening: Listen to your franchisees' concerns without trying to defend yourself. Instead, work with them to find solutions and convince them that these changes are for the better. Don't forget that change is an additional stress for them.

   Simplify again and again: Help franchisees order changes within their franchise. Do everything in your power to simplify the change process and make it as easy as possible to implement.

2. **Enable franchisees to take ownership of the change by achieving their own objectives within the strategy.** For many franchisees, your strategic plan won't be concrete. I've often heard people say, "Those are nice words and ideas, but what's in it for me? How much is it going to cost me?"

   As part of your planning, you should hold working sessions with your franchisees and create with them a plan for success, maximizing the effects of your strategy.

   One of the best ways to do this is to help them create their own success plan based on the action plan's objectives.

   This joint effort will enable them to achieve the objectives of your proposed plan.

3. **Take responsibility.**
   If I were your coach, you'd never be able to tell me that it's the franchisees' fault that your plan isn't working. As a leader, you must accept complete responsibility for your results. Your integrity is at stake.

   Organize your priorities around your strategic plan and use the formula for success to better visualize your success. Invest time in the field with your franchisees to see the effects of the plan. Although you need to remain flexible in applying your plan, it's up to you to make sure your franchisees succeed.

If your results aren't what you expected, don't hesitate to work with your franchisees to find solutions. They're the ones who have your success in their hands, even more than you think.

Deploy your strategic plan by implementing these three key actions to engage your franchisees:

a. **Navigate the chaos of change**
   - Acknowledging fear: Change can be intimidating for your franchisees. Anticipate their reactions and be prepared to support them.
   - Active listening: Open a sincere dialogue. Don't just impose, listen and work with your franchisees to overcome obstacles together.
   - Simplification: Facilitate the adoption of changes by making them as simple as possible. Offer new training courses and provide easy-to-follow steps for integrating new practices.

b. **Involve franchisees in the strategy**
   - Make the plan concrete: Organize workshops to transform your strategy into personalized action plans for each franchisee.
   - Collaborative planning: Work hand-in-hand with franchisees so they can see how your strategy translates into success for their business.

c. **Assume your role as a responsible leader**
- No excuses: As a leader, you are fully accountable for results. Take a proactive approach and avoid blaming franchisees.
- Focus on the field: Invest time with your franchisees. Observe the impact of your strategy in the field, and remain flexible to adapt it if necessary.
- Find solutions together: If results aren't living up to your expectations, work with your franchisees to identify and solve the problems. Remember that their success contributes directly to yours.

By following these steps, you'll position your franchise network for shared, lasting success based on a relationship of trust and collaboration.

Putting Your Strategic Impact Plan into Action

You want to make changes to create or recreate the network you want, with franchisees who are committed and ready to do whatever it takes to realize the full potential of their business. Here's how.

1. **Develop a robust deployment plan**
   Launching your new strategic plan and asserting your leadership within your network requires a major effort on your part. I often see uncoordinated initiatives on both sides, and quite frankly, they're a dead end.

By drawing up a deployment plan, you'll be able to do this more easily. Your deployment should capitalize on the influence of your leaders within your company.

5 STEPS OF STRATEGIC PLAN COMMUNICATION

MANAGEMENT TEAM + SHAREHOLDERS
1 2 3 4 5
FRANCHISOR TEAM
SEASONED FRANCHISEES
FRANCHISE NETWORK AT LARGE
FRANCHISE NETWORK ECOSYSTEM

Circle 1: Management team, shareholders
Circle 2: Network support and operations teams
Circle 3: Outstanding franchisees
Circle 4: Franchise network
Circle 5: Your network's ecosystem (suppliers, strategic players)

Your priority: Get the full buy-in of your leadership team and your franchisees.

2. **Launch your new initiative with full force**
   This effort must be initiated in a **spectacular** way (I stress the word **spectacular**, as franchisors often make the mistake of not forcefully demonstrating not only the expected results, but also the benefits of the plans proposed to franchisees). Remember that group morale develops through shared experiences and the results of our efforts. Of course, this effort must continue to be supported on a regular basis by all team members, as well as by reinforcement activities.

   Once Circles 1, 2, and 3 have been informed, we suggest you organize a conference-type event.

   The aim: to get everyone on the same wavelength. By making a public commitment, you'll motivate the troops!

   Use this event to inspire change. Inviting a guest speaker can be a good way of preparing for the event and opening up everyone's mind.

   You can also host a brainstorming activity at your event. You could ask participants (in small groups of 8 to 12) to answer the question: how are you going to achieve this or that objective (I prefer non-financial objectives, to free up as much creativity as possible)? In this way, you'll encourage franchisees to take ownership of your objectives.

3. **Perform quarterly and annual follow-ups**

   Stay the course and report on the progress of your plan to your entire organization. You'll be surprised at the effect on the Effort component of the success formula. Whether the results are good or bad, by remaining transparent, you'll gain credibility through your integrity. Your leadership will be all the better for it.

   Also, every time a target is reached, communicate the news to your franchisees, preferably by sending a video message, not a written one. A video will better convey the message—and the feelings associated with success. Don't forget to CELEBRATE!

4. **Communicate, again and again!**

   They say you have to repeat a message seven times before it's really understood. This is even truer in the context of a strategic plan.

   Create a simple message that sums up the plan, and make sure EVERYONE communicates it regularly. Your vision, mission, and values need to be repeated and discussed as often as possible.

   As for the objectives, this will depend on whether all the members of your network adhere to them and take the actions required at their level to achieve them.

What's Next?

Now you're ready to implement your plan and become a franchise leader who makes an impact in your network. You're clear about what you're proposing (which makes everyone feel secure), and you're taking action to put in place the building blocks of your franchise's success formula.

The Challenge of Managing Change Within a Franchise Network

"If you don't take change by the hand, it will take you by the throat."

– Winston Churchill

The V.U.C.A. world is forcing increasingly rapid and far-reaching changes within franchise networks. This is evidenced by the technological revolution, concept changes to meet new needs, and evolving business models...

Franchisees seem to be the main obstacle to innovation. But in fact, it's not so much up to them as it is up to you.

In this chapter, we talked about resistance to change and how to reduce it.

I'd now like to introduce you to a method for managing change effectively.

Inadequate change management is a major factor in:

- Creation of franchisee associations
- Acceleration of turnover rate
- Creation of passive-aggressive behavior and non-commitment on the part of franchisees who adopt the change with regret or under pressure from the franchisor

Why is change so difficult in franchise networks?

Studies show that 70% of changes fail to produce the desired results. In today's V.U.C.A. environment, you won't survive long if you don't learn to manage change effectively.

There are several reasons for this:

1. **Franchisees don't understand**
   Despite your best efforts, your franchisees don't fully understand your strategy or the change you want to make. In this case, simply ask them, "Can you explain to me what you understand about the change I'm proposing?" You'll be amazed at the answers. Indeed, when a franchisee doesn't understand, they tend to interpret proposed changes negatively. If this is the case, go back to your formula for success (Faith, Focus, Effort) and identify what's not working with them. A word of advice: stay humble.

2. **They don't see the benefit of changing**
   Franchisors tend to underestimate the importance of showing tangible evidence of the benefits the requested

changes will bring. Real-life case studies with willing franchisees, potential profitability scenarios, market studies, and other demonstrations of the results of proposed initiatives are the best way to cut through the arguments and allow franchisees to see the short- and medium-term benefits.

3. **They are unable to cope with change**
   Unfortunately, I see this situation on a regular basis. There are two types of disability:

   a. **Lack of competence**
      This situation deserves special attention, as it is a major obstacle. Franchisees often don't dare tell you that they don't know how to integrate change into their franchise. A personalized assessment and training approach is the best solution.

   b. **Lack of financial resources**
      This is a real problem that stops change and growth in its tracks. We need to distinguish between a temporary cash-flow problem and a lack of profitability.

In the latter case, the only option is to make every effort to turn around profitability so that the franchisee can make the changes with confidence. If the situation proves impossible to rectify, you'll need to take steps to minimize the damage on both sides. Prolonging the problem can have serious consequences for the brand.

If the change involves a major investment, and cash flow is unable to support it, you'll need to set up a financing program with a lender. In some cases, temporary financing may be the solution.

In short, never underestimate resistance to change.

According to J.P. Kotter, author of the book *Leading Change*, change can succeed if you avoid the following mistakes:

Mistake 1: You haven't established a sufficient sense of urgency.

Human beings don't like change. They only change if it's really necessary. It's the same with franchisees. So you need to create a sense of urgency. There's no point in shouting out that there is a fire if there's no fire, but it is necessary to make franchisees understand that a change made today will avoid this or that problem tomorrow and the day after tomorrow.

The use of expert studies can be of great help in promoting this urgency.

Mistake 2: You haven't set up a strong enough guiding coalition.

As a network leader, you have to think in coalition. Playing Superman won't do you any good. You'll wear yourself out.

1. Make sure your entire team is with you to implement your plan.
2. Federate the best elements so that they support you and serve as a pillar of credibility to facilitate the commitment

of other franchisees. A word of advice: take the time to do it properly, just to make sure all the pieces fit together.

Mistake 3: The vision of the future isn't clear enough.

You're too much into tactics and details.

In fact, you lack vision and are unable to help franchisees project themselves into the future by adopting the changes you propose. This increases insecurity. The result: your franchisees resist even more.

Mistake 4: You don't communicate your vision enough.

The foundation of your strategic plan and the changes you want to make is your vision. But it's all too easy to forget your vision. Stephen Covey, in his book *The Seven Habits of Highly Effective People*, says, "Begin with the end in mind."

Apply this approach to all of your communications. The vision should be at the heart of every conversation, every meeting, every encounter. Don't hesitate to use every means at your disposal to communicate it effectively. The message will get through, believe me!

Mistake 5: You haven't identified the obstacles preventing your new vision from becoming a reality.

Let's face it, a new vision is a bit like the title of Mr. Goldsmith's book *What Got You Here Won't Get You There*. If you want to change things, you have to put the resources in place to do so.

For the franchisor, this may mean new investments, new resources, and new lines of business. For franchisees, it's much the same. By identifying the obstacles that stand in the way of achieving the plan's objectives, and taking steps to overcome or minimize them, change will be easier.

Mistake 6: You haven't planned for or created short-term gains.

Short-term gains are very important for accelerating change because they give franchisees security and motivate them to keep going. So it's imperative that your planning takes them into account. Realistically, in the eyes of a franchisee, the first six months of a new strategic plan sets the tone, the first year sets the pace. Year 2 brings long-term benefits, and year 3 combines all the initiatives and secures the profits.

For the franchisor, the real benefits come in the medium term. A critical mass must have implemented the proposed changes to see the results. Perseverance is an important asset in managing change.

Of course, in the case of changing physical concepts, contractual obligations may slow down implementation, but this should be foreseen in the plan.

Mistake 7: You declared victory too soon.

Yogi Berra said, "It's not over until it's over." It's the same with the execution of your plan. Neglecting to maintain tempo, underestimating the energy and resources to get to the end of the plan, assuming franchisees are still committed, you name it. Be vigilant.

Mistake 8: You haven't anchored the changes in the network culture.

It's your job to make sure the changes are integrated into the network's culture. To do this, you need to measure progress and results in a systematic way, to keep you on track with your new vision. This will be the subject of Chapter 10.

Conclusion

In the V.U.C.A. world of franchising, effective change management is crucial. Adopting a methodical approach, actively involving and supporting franchisees, and systematically measuring progress is essential.

Coach's Thoughts

Moving from reflection to action is a demanding exercise.

The first phase is a communication exercise, not an advertising campaign to persuade. This process involves working with franchisees so that they feel able to implement this new strategy through this new action plan.

Don't neglect individual integration work, otherwise your group exercise will be a waste of time. The Franchisee Success Action Plan is the ideal tool for getting franchisees on board, and above all for taking quality time with them to talk about the future. Want to know more and find solutions? Check for the bonus pack you can receive by using the QR code on page 6.

"Strategy without tactics is the slowest route to victory. Tactics without strategy is the noise before defeat."

— Sun Tzu

Chapter 10

Without Feedback, the Strategic Plan Is Useless

The success of a strategic plan depends on its execution. What's more, if you don't include feedback from franchisees, you'll be going in blind. Building an effective feedback system that's neither too heavy nor too light will take time, technology, and collaboration.

Here's how to build the system.

Structure Your Feedback Plan with a Dashboard

1. **The key to success: The dashboard**
   Create a dashboard that goes far beyond simple numbers. It must reflect the overall health of your business, your franchisees, and the effectiveness of your strategic plan. Think of it as the cockpit of your airplane; all the vital information you need to fly successfully.

2. **Performance indicators that speak for themselves**
   Choose KPIs (key performance indicators) that address the essential aspects of your network. These indicators should be aligned with your strategic priorities. Don't just measure for the sake of measuring. Each KPI must have a clear purpose and be directly linked to your objectives.

3. **What to measure**
   Use tools like Franchise Performance 360© to inspire you and tailor your KPIs to your unique needs. There is no universal magic formula; what counts is creating KPIs that reflect your reality.

4. **Don't lose sight of your action plan**
   An effective dashboard does more than just observe: it must be an active management tool. Include a project tracking section. Make sure that each project is progressing according to plan. Remember that when implementing a strategic plan, time is of the essence.

5. **Agility and constant updates**
   Your dashboard must be dynamic. Update it regularly, and make sure your team and franchisees are in tune with the information it contains. An outdated dashboard is as useless as a rudderless boat.

   Appoint a dashboard custodian. His or her role will be to check that information is submitted and validated on time.

6. **Commitment through transparency**

   Share your dashboard with your franchisees. This will establish a culture of transparency and commitment. If your franchisees understand where the network is heading and how they contribute to its success, their motivation and commitment will increase tenfold.

7. **Efficient meetings**

   Use your dashboard at strategy meetings. Discussions will be more focused, and you'll be able to quickly identify areas requiring special attention so you can make informed decisions.

8. **Celebrate success**

   Use the dashboard to recognize and celebrate successes. For example, when a franchisee meets or exceeds a key KPI, let other franchisees know. This will reinforce the performance culture within your network.

9. **Evolution and adaptation**

   Your network evolves, your market changes. Your dashboard must reflect this evolution. Be ready to adjust your KPIs in line with new market realities and your network's objectives.

10. **Training and support**

    Provide your team and franchisees with the training they need to understand and use the dashboard effectively. A poorly understood tool is a poorly used tool.

In short, a well-designed dashboard is a powerful tool. It provides you with a clear global vision, helps you make strategic decisions, and keeps the whole team rowing in the same direction.

Leverage the Power of Franchisee Feedback to Energize the Strategic Plan

Catch signals in the field: Your franchisees are your eyes and ears in the field. Actively encourage them to share their observations and experiences. Their feedback is a goldmine for refining and adjusting your strategy in real-time.

Involve to innovate: Turn every franchisee into a key player in the plan's success. By participating in the decision-making process, they bring not only their local expertise, but also their commitment to making the plan a success. It's a win-win collaboration.

Open dialogue, reinforced trust: Establish an ongoing dialogue with franchisees. Show them that their voice counts, and that it can have a real influence on overall strategy. This is the foundation of lasting trust and a solid franchisee-franchisor relationship.

For example, one client is using a dedicated email address (Tellme@ABCfranchise.com) to give the franchisees direct access to him.

Adapt in real-time: Be agile and responsive to feedback. Markets evolve rapidly, and franchisees in the field are often the first to detect these changes. Use their observations to react quickly.

Prevent problems: Don't let small worries turn into big obstacles. Use franchisee feedback to identify and resolve problems quickly, before they escalate.

Value every contribution: Every comment is an opportunity to strengthen the brand and improve operations. Recognizing and valuing franchisees' contributions creates an environment conducive to innovation and continuous improvement.

Measure and celebrate success: Use franchisee feedback to measure the effectiveness of the plan, and celebrate successes. This will boost morale and motivate the entire network to continue their efforts on the road to success.

Mobilize for change: Show franchisees that their observations contribute directly to shaping a better future. Involve them in the implementation of change, so that they feel part of it and motivated.

In sum: Franchisees' comments and observations are not just a measurement tool. They are a powerful lever for action and innovation. By harnessing them, you'll build a dynamic, adaptable, and unified network, ready to meet market challenges and seize opportunities.

Why Rely on Your Franchisees to Implement the Plan?

1. **Build solid trust:** Be transparent in your strategies. Show your franchisees that you are committed and open. Clear communication creates a climate of mutual trust essential to success.

2. **Real responsibility:** Show that you take responsibility. This will motivate your franchisees to invest themselves fully and feel equally responsible for the network's success.

3. **Continuous improvement:** Listen to your franchisees' feedback. Use their observations to refine your strategies and respond effectively to market needs.

4. **Strong strategic alignment:** Make sure your franchisees understand and support your decisions. An aligned network is a strong network.

5. **Create value for all:** Let your franchisees understand how the strategy benefits the whole network, including their own businesses.

6. **Anticipate and manage conflicts:** Be proactive. Regular communication helps detect and resolve problems before they escalate.

7. **Reinforce commitment:** Show that you value your franchisees' opinions. This will increase their commitment and motivation.

In concrete terms:

- Hold regular meetings to discuss strategy with franchisees
- Create feedback channels through which franchisees can express their opinions and suggestions
- Set up training workshops to help franchisees understand and integrate the strategy
- Develop clear performance indicators and share results regularly
- Encourage franchisee initiatives that are in line with the overall strategy

Remember, the success of a franchise network depends as much on the franchisor's vision as on the commitment of each franchisee. Your role is to guide, listen, and act for the common success.

Coach's Thoughts

The feedback stage is one that is often overlooked when I'm working with customers using the Franchisexcel© system. Yet it's very useful and will help you avoid making the same mistakes.

By taking the time not to skip this step, you increase your chances of satisfying franchisees. Indeed, beyond plans, Key Performance Indicators (KPIs) and big meetings, it's their opinion that will bring you closer to their reality and their ability to execute the plan.

To make sure you don't forget this step, you should set up feedback-related KPIs. That way, you can keep track of them on your dashboard.

"To take a 'see no evil, hear no evil' approach is worthless. I want to hear where the issues are and then address what we are going to do about them."

— Dave Mattson, CEO, Sandler Training

Part 3

Practical Case Studies – The Best and the Worst

Chapter 11

Transforming a Network in Decline: The Test of Resilience and Leadership

Background:

A[7] is a regional franchisor of specialized quick-service restaurants. At the time of my client's acquisition, the network consisted of some twenty branches, 12 of which were corporate. The brand was already 20 years old and had not been able to expand. The team that acquired the franchise is very young, but has experience in franchising, having been a multiple franchisee of a major international brand. The buyer is very familiar with the state of the network, having been a franchisee for several years.

Profits are minimal due to disappointing sales performance, non-existent management controls, and laxity in both company restaurants and franchises.

The first year was devoted to financial recovery in order to restore minimum profitability. In the second year, management decided

---

[7]   The client's name is kept confidential for competitive reasons.

to work with me to help them turn the corner for the next phase of growth.

Interesting fact: The current team is highly skilled in restaurant management, and well versed in the success factors that a brand needs to succeed. Here, we're co-creating the franchise of the future, not the concept of the future. The growth leadership exercise offered by Franchisexcel© is highly relevant.

Problem #1: The Formula for Success is Not Well-Defined

Even if the management team knows what to do to turn the company around, they don't know how to act when faced with the challenge of franchise growth. The key to the success of the new strategy is to focus on the diagnosis proposed by Franchise Performance 360© and then define the formula for success (Faith, Focus, Effort).

By clarifying the ingredients of the formula, we can set out a three-year strategic plan to not only double the size of the network, but also create a world-class franchise network capable of supporting accelerated growth.

The vision is finally clear, and the path to get there is described step by step.

One of the challenges is to build a management team capable of delivering the goods. Indeed, the new strategy highlights the lack of quality resources and the need to specialize in those that are present. The era of the all-purpose employee who is good at nothing has lasted long enough.

I'd like to congratulate the CEO for her courage. At the time, she made the decision to reduce the franchisor's short-term profitability so that she could add new team members and go ahead with the plan.

Problem #2: Existing Franchisees

This new strategy calls for operational excellence in order to develop significant organic growth and enable expansion at lower risk. As you know, working with new franchisees is easier than working with existing ones.

Many parts of the Franchisexcel© system are applied in a disciplined way, as existing franchisees are very resistant. Used to fend for themselves and not rely on the franchisor (previously absent from their daily lives), they have to adapt to a proactive, willing, and creative franchisor. This is no easy task.

Management decided to focus on the success formula (Faith, Focus, Effort) and create a new culture. The aim is to enable all franchisees to grow together. As for the franchisor, they must be able to capitalize on all his franchisees. Although still in its infancy, this approach will create a strong alignment that will force some franchisees to question their future in the network. The approach should not be coercive; rather based on requirements that are known and integrated by all. Thanks to this new culture, the company will be able to embark on its new growth without looking back.

This will take time and effort, but management is convinced that this is the way forward to ensure that all network forces are pulling in the same direction.

Major Results

1. **Return to profitability**

    As a result of the management team's hard work during the first year, the company became profitable at levels consistent with its size. Drawing on its expertise, the management team quickly solved the main problems affecting sales. They were not afraid to take on project after project. A new image, innovations, customer activation activities, a focus on operational fundamentals, and increasingly assertive leadership: this was the recipe for the turnaround.

2. **A stronger management team**

    Despite the profitability stakes, the CEO still takes the risk of hiring the right resources to implement the basic plan for the next three years and exercise her true role as CEO of a franchise network.

3. **Clarity**

    From a situation of reactive urgency, the company is moving to a situation of proactivity, which lays the foundations for phase 2 of the plan (creating and implementing the new culture of operational excellence).

4. **Franchisee confidence grows by the day**
   Lack of trust is a franchisor's biggest expense. However, the team's proactivity has enabled it to win back the trust of older franchisees (even if the hardest part is yet to come). What's more, this confidence is reflected in the creation of six new franchises in the second year.

5. **A more solid base to face the challenges of growth**
   Although the new culture is not yet fully integrated, the network's health signals are almost all in the green. This new foundation will enable the company to accelerate its growth with minimal risk.

Stay tuned!

Coach's Thoughts

Turning around a franchise network is a perilous exercise. All too often, it's just a matter of changing the image, the concept, and the advertising campaign. History is replete with the lack of success of these overrated turnarounds. While these aspects are important, success doesn't just happen. The culture of the company and its network must change, and franchisees must adopt it. Here are a few thoughts that might help you avoid your network turnaround being a beautiful stillborn project.

1. **It's urgent to do nothing; it's time to plan**
   Your network's recipe for success depends on your strategic alignment. The Franchisexcel© system has been created with this in mind: the discipline it demands is designed to leave no blind spots and help you chart your course towards the future you want.

2. **Quick wins are very important to encourage buy-in to the changes you are proposing**
   See Chapter 9 for more details. These successful quick wins must be planned and integrated into the deployment of your new strategy. Without them, the "secret sauce" of your success formula will take much longer to set.

3. **Be demanding, but not harsh**
   The most respected leaders are demanding leaders. The same applies to franchisors. But don't confuse demanding with strict. Severity implies exercising authoritarian power. I'd even go so far as to say that it demotivates and makes franchisees passive-aggressive ("I'll say yes, but I won't do

it"). At best, things move forward when you're present, but as soon as your back is turned, everything goes back to the way it was before.

On the contrary, being demanding calls for you to go beyond yourself, to have the courage to change, to invest in growth, and to reject the status quo. *"What got you here won't get you there,"* as Goldsmith puts it, is the mindset required of a demanding franchisee. In my opinion, it's this demand that defines leadership.

Chapter 12

Creating an Exceptional Franchise Network by Empowering Franchisees

Background:

B[8], a network of fast-food franchises, is on a roll. The first franchise was launched in 2012. Over the past five years, organic growth has been between 15% and 25% year on year. Annual network growth of over 50%. Franchisees and franchisors alike are profitable. The business model is extremely successful. B is the darling of real estate developers. The shareholders are extremely committed and have North American ambitions. However, they realize that their way of doing things is not sustainable in the long term. B's strength lies in its attention to quality in both product and operations, and its willingness to deliver the goods to franchisees.

But the strategic question is how to achieve exponential growth while maintaining exceptional product and operational quality standards.

---

[8] The client's name is kept confidential for competitive reasons.

Problem #1: A Control-Oriented Culture that Defines Franchises as Mere Operators

Aside from the usual problems of a growing network, the Franchise Performance 360© analysis highlights the detrimental effect of the network's initial culture, which puts control at the forefront. It forces the franchisor to invest too many resources in this area, and disempowers the franchisee.

This culture generates friction within the franchisor-franchisee relationship, does not give franchisees enough responsibility for their success, and sub-optimizes the franchisor's value creation by forcing him to create a cumbersome and not very proactive operational structure.

Solutions

A control-first culture significantly slows growth and doesn't improve performance. Using various elements of Franchisexcel©, we co-create the B-franchisor of the future. I intentionally skip the elements of budget planning and creating better KPIs to focus on the power of redefining B's formula for success (Faith, Focus, Effort). Indeed, the management team decided to give the franchisee maximum responsibility by creating a growth model based solely on multiple merit-based franchises.

This requires significant investment to enable franchisees to take on their new responsibilities.

B now focuses on the human factor, while developing a demanding yet empowering culture. Franchisees are now growth-oriented business partners, and the franchisor's team works, not for franchisees, but with them.

Problem #2: Building the Team for the Future

The new strategic plan highlights the inability to achieve objectives without creating an even more competent team. Indeed, by focusing on the human factor instead of system fundamentals, priorities are reversed.

This choice underlines the importance of skills development being aligned with mission, values, and leadership, rather than prioritizing technical skills.

Solutions

The initial training program has been revised and extended. The franchisor now offers a University of B by regional markets, to create the franchisees of the future, but also to continue developing existing franchisees. For the first time in five years, it is organizing an annual convention. The theme: Excellence. No excuses. Communication rituals are now established and in place.

The other priority is to define who can be part of the team before establishing new roles and responsibilities.

The team is divided into three.

In addition to the normal criteria and those specific to the company's culture, each team component now has three specific criteria focusing on the human qualities sought.

- Franchisees: Field leader, team player, proactive
- The operational team: A mobilizing leader, superior emotional intelligence, highly skilled in business management
- The support team: Strategic, team player, mobilizing leader—not a power leader

The projects to achieve excellence have been spread over the three years of the plan to ensure optimum implementation.

The Results

In just 12 months, thanks to the iron will of the current management team, results are being seen at every level of the network.

1. **Culture change**
   The new, empowering culture retains the good elements of the past, while driving up operational quality scores and sales development initiatives in local markets. Now, it's the franchisees who do their own performance audits and work with the success coach to improve. Most of the work is about identifying solutions, not problems. The effect of this new culture is to galvanize the franchisor's support team, while mobilizing franchisees around the vision and values that are "The 10 non-negotiable rules at B."

2. **Strategic focus**
   Following the results of Franchisexcel©, decisions are made based on values, strategy, and key objectives. This forces important choices to be made which, without the

plan, would have been low-return initiatives (what I call false good ideas).

3. **Discipline based on results, not effort**
   This new culture emphasizes the importance of results, not just effort. It forces everyone in the network to deliver the expected results without excuses or prevarication. Team spirit is strong, and mutual support is omnipresent. In fact, those who can't embrace this culture leave on their own.

4. **Increased quality**
   By making franchisees accountable for their results, quality levels rise significantly. In fact, the idea of making franchisees responsible for performance audits has made everyone aware of everything that goes into creating operational excellence. Training needs arise at all levels. Complacency is no longer the order of the day.

5. **Accelerating growth**
   By freeing themselves from the burden of a control culture, franchisors can accelerate their growth plans. What's more, with a merit-based multi-franchise program, franchisees raise their hands to embark on new adventures. One of the most important results is the revision of the growth targets set out in the initial plan. Year 3 of the plan becomes Year 2, while Year 3 calls for the growth of one new franchise per week. It's easy to see the value creation from this approach. In three years, B will have over 150 franchises in operation, five times the initial number.

Imagine the next strategic plan!

Coach's Thoughts

This story can be yours if your fundamentals are strong enough and your desire for growth unwavering. Here are a few questions to ask yourself before embarking on a major growth plan:

Q1: How can you transform your franchisees' perception so that instead of seeing themselves as mere operators, they see themselves as genuine, committed business partners?

Q2: What concrete strategies will you put in place to ensure that growth does not come at the expense of product and operational quality?

Q3: What measures will you adopt to reinforce the competence and commitment of your management team and franchisees, so that their objectives are in line with those of the franchise network?

Chapter 13

From Corporate to Franchise Model

Background:

C[9] specializes in residential energy optimization. It runs successful corporate branches. The company is active in Eastern Canada and Florida in the U.S.

C is highly skilled in customer acquisition, thanks to a door-to-door representation strategy. The team is young and very sales-oriented. It has developed an extremely efficient development methodology and systems. It is convinced that its success depends on the human factor. The company therefore wants to change its business model to a franchise model.

It aims to become a major player in this market, but lacks the resources to accelerate its growth exponentially in other sectors.

The question: How do you transform yourself into a franchise without risking losing everything?

---

[9]   The client's name must be kept confidential for competitive reasons.

Problem #1: Understanding the Implications of the Decision

Although the decision to transform the company into a franchise business has been taken, I must emphasize the determination of the shareholders and management to get it right. The biggest problem is that no one on the management team knows what is involved in transforming the business model. This creates insecurity and affects performance.

Solutions

We use Franchise Performance 360© to carry out a complete assessment and diagnosis of the organization.

By taking the time to analyze each point, the management team is able to grasp all the dimensions of the business model and identify current shortcomings as well as possible solutions. Given the scale of the project and the associated risks, the company decided to postpone its changeover for 12 months, to prepare itself adequately.

The biggest challenge of this preparation: creating more value for the network and empowering future franchisees to be more autonomous in their success. Following a geomarketing analysis, all territories were reorganized, and the current market potential doubled.

As far as autonomy is concerned, although the systems in place are efficient, they were not designed to operate in the decentralized mode required by franchising. For example, the coordination of installation projects for equipment sold is centralized. In a franchise, however, this coordination must be decentralized in order to ensure franchisee control and enhance service quality. Also, at the sales level, management is centralized, and branch managers have only a coordinating and training role. In a franchise, however, sales management belongs to the franchisees, and they are fully responsible for the results.

The first 12 months of the plan are devoted to putting in place the fundamentals of a successful franchise system and building a more competent franchise team.

Problem #2: From an SME Culture to a Mindset of a High-Growth Organization

The franchisor's role is to maximize their and their franchisees' growth in order to create the desired value. To do this, typical SME management reflexes don't apply so well. Control is not at the same level, and franchise partners don't react to challenges in the same way as a manager. Running a network is different from running an SME. What's more, it's not innate in entrepreneurs. Often, the failure of a franchise network stems from the way leaders work with franchisees, not from the business model or even performance.

Solutions

To achieve the desired culture change, we used the Franchisexcel© system to establish a consistent strategic plan and a new culture. The method established strategic alignment and a detailed plan, and enabled franchisor leaders and managers to take ownership of their new roles and responsibilities. The exercise also revealed that 50% of current managers cannot become franchisees.

The Results

Although implementation is recent, the following results have been observed:

1. Better cohesion within the franchisor's team, thanks to clarification of roles and responsibilities.

2. The CEO focuses on developing the company and the new culture. To this end, they have put in place very precise rituals to ensure the vitality of the culture of growth and empowerment of leaders within the network.

3. Managers who have been converted to franchisees are producing better-than-expected results.

4. The quality of customer service has improved.

5. C University has become the place to develop leadership skills, not just a sales school.

6. For the duration of the plan, development in the U.S. is focused on a single market.

7. In order to gain experience before launching the National U.S. franchisor, market development is carried out with partners who may, if they wish, become franchisees when the company becomes a franchisor in the U.S.

8. The franchisee recruitment plan is used to focus on candidates from within the network (inbreeding). Now, as part of our growth strategy, we also accept applications from outside the network.

9. To increase market share in new territories, the franchisor implements a customer acquisition strategy that includes inbound marketing.

Conclusion

The company is now a fully-fledged franchisor. Growth is in the cards, thanks to the determination of the leaders and the Franchisexcel© system, which has eliminated the risk of transition and preserved the value developed. The implementation of the new culture is going well, and customers are more satisfied than ever.

Coach's Thoughts

This case illustrates that major changes are often necessary within franchise networks. These often have to go beyond the physical concept. Here, it's a question of adopting a new business model without sacrificing value, but rather increasing it in an accelerated mode. To make this change, you need to ask yourself the following questions:

Understanding the new model:

- Have you clearly assessed the impact the changes will have on your current business model?
- What aspects of your current business model will require adaptation or transformation?
- How do you plan to prepare and support your team and franchisees through this significant change?

Change management and leadership:

- How do you plan to manage cultural change so that your franchisees adopt the new business model with confidence?
- What specific challenges do you face in the leadership and management of franchise partners?
- Do you have a plan for developing the new management and leadership skills you, your management team, and franchisees will need?

Conclusion

We Don't Have 200 Years to Build Thriving Franchise Networks

In the face of the constant change brought by the V.U.C.A. world, you are now faced with a choice: whether or not to follow the leadership path I propose. By adopting impactful leadership behaviors, you will be able to extend your influence far beyond franchise conventions or operation manuals. It's time to reprogram your mindset toward franchising.

Your network needs you as a leader, not just a manager.

Too often, franchisors do just enough to keep things running. It's as if they see their role merely as service providers and motivators. Sure, that's fine, but it all becomes purely transactional, and franchisees are viewed as business partners, nothing more.

However, to create a world-class network (even if you don't intend to expand beyond your country's borders), you must go further. The leadership behaviors I suggest in Franchise Performance 360© are a solid foundation, but the magic ingredient of your success formula is heart... Yes, heart. What truly drives franchisees to excel isn't money: it's the desire for self-fulfillment. And this desire is born from answering the following three questions:

- Is my franchisor competent?
- Am I respected as a franchisee?
- Can I trust my franchisor?

Without this security, the heart simply won't be in it. Sure, you'll do business, and probably good business, but you'll never reach the full potential you desire without developing the human side of your business relationship. It's a shame for leaders who believe franchising is just about making money.

With Franchisexcel©, you can achieve this because it provides the roadmap to:

Increase:

- The skills that create success for both the franchisor and the franchisees.
- The connection and team spirit within the network.
- The culture of excellence that builds trust.

Eliminate:

- The defeatist attitude that stems from a lack of connection.
- The fear of success by tolerating mediocrity.
- The lack of commitment to the network's mission and values.

See Franchisexcel© as a platform that will allow you to reinvent your franchise by revisiting the very foundations of your partnership with your franchisees.

By working with the Franchisexcel© system, you give yourself permission to reimagine your impact on your franchisees and let your imagination soar.

Franchisexcel© can be the path that enables you to unlock your network's full potential and fulfill your original dream: to expand your brand into all possible markets with strong franchise partners, while realizing the full economic and human value of your incredible journey.

Franchisexcel© will help you tackle the major challenges of today's V.U.C.A. world:

Creating value beyond just economic gains (I must stress this again)

Needs and values have evolved. The human factor is more critical than ever within your network. By considering your franchisees as part of a community rather than just business partners, you contribute to their personal growth, allowing them to excel in their communities and within your network.

Ensuring the longevity of your network

Everything moves faster now. You must find ways to create a culture that embraces change, loves technology, and is willing to test innovations based on ROI, not just sales.

Evolving the business model to share collective wealth

Franchisees are business partners: they invest in their success, but also in your brand. Ask yourself the real questions, such as:

- What can you do to better share the wealth that franchisees help you build?
- What is your responsibility in your franchisees' personal development so they can surpass their limits and achieve even greater success in life?
- How can you create this culture of infinite growth within your network?

By providing concrete answers to these questions, you will increase your impact as an exceptional leader for your franchisees.

This is Only a Goodbye

I sincerely hope that this book has sparked in you the desire for a new growth culture based on leadership within your network. This culture values not only growth but also human development through a franchise success model.

Wishing you great success, and see you soon!

Stéphane

About the Author

Stéphane Breault, MBA
Executive coach for network CEOs and franchise consultant

Stéphane Breault has been CEO of Canadian franchise networks for two decades and a franchise expert for over 15 years. With his vast experience in franchise management, he has forged a singular and personal vision of the sector. So, unlike many franchise consultants who focus on the technical and tactical aspects of the business, Stéphane works with CEOs and executives to help them become exceptional franchisors who value strong partnerships with franchisees.

Stéphane is renowned for his strategic and creative approach. His straightforward approach provokes the emergence of ideas that become the basis for practical solutions that can be easily implemented. Moreover, he combines pragmatic experience with methods that motivate his customers to open up and get involved.

Stéphane has advised over 100 Canadian and international franchise networks. He has helped them plan their growth, rethink their business models, and develop leadership within their management teams. He has also provided them with the relevant tools to implement a culture of operational excellence and expand internationally.

Stéphane is a past president of the Canadian Franchise Association and the Québec MBA Association. In January 2018, he was elected to the Québec Franchise Council's Hall of Fame. He also sits on the Board of Directors of the Conseil québécois de la franchise.

About Imagine Franchise Consultant Inc.

Founded in 2018, Imagine Franchise supports franchisors in an emerging phase or facing growth challenges that threaten the network's value creation potential. Through its Franchisexcel© program, it works hand-in-hand with CEOs and management teams to RE-align, RE-imagine, RE-develop, and RE-organize their network, and MAXIMIZE value creation for both franchisees and franchisors.

Its approach is resolutely personalized, whether in executive coaching for CEOs and their teams, the definition of new strategies, or leadership development within management teams and franchisees.

www.ingramcontent.com/pod-product-compliance
Lightning Source LLC
Chambersburg PA
CBHW071553200326
41519CB00021BB/6724